Monographs on communication technology and utilization 2

Titles in the series

1. *Super 8: the modest medium*
2. *Film animation: a simplified approach*
3. *Audio cassettes: the user medium*
4. *VTR workshop: small format video*

Film animation: a simplified approach

John Halas

Published in 1976 by the United Nations
Educational, Scientific and Cultural
Organization
7 Place de Fontenoy, 75700 Paris
Printed by Imprimeries Réunies S.A., Lausanne

ISBN 92-3-101367-X

Preface

This publication is the second in an occasional series of monographs commissioned by Unesco on practical aspects of communication technology. Their purpose is to synthesize and share technical information as soon as it has reached a reliable stage of experimentation. Obviously, it is difficult to forecast in advance trends and titles for such a rapidly changing field, but the monograph series seeks to treat from time to time those topics considered most urgent, most viable, and most relevant to the needs of the developing world.

This monograph is concerned with film animation, traditionally a highly technical and skilled art requiring precision equipment and costly talents. It is not a how-to book for beginners, but a presentation of basic animation techniques for those already familiar with film-making. Through the proposed short cuts in time, materials, and facilities, it is hoped that smaller production teams working with modest budgets can also tap the potential of film animation.

The author of the monograph is John Halas who for many years produced and directed animated films in London, New York and Paris. He also directed, with Joy Batchelor, *Animal Farm*, the first full-length animated feature film in the United Kingdom. Author of several books on film animation, he is currently Director of the Educational Film Centre Ltd. in London, and President of the Association Internationale des Films d'Animation (the International Animated Film Association) involving thirty-six nations.

The chapter on the 'Production of Animation' was largely compiled by Brian Salt, a well-known rostrum camera expert.

Other titles soon to follow in this series will deal with portable videotape production and audiocassette operations.

The opinions expressed in this study are those of the author and do not necessarily reflect those of Unesco.

Contents

Chapter I

Basic principles of animation

Film animation is a highly complex form of activity involving a combination of intellect and skill, plus a high degree of creativity. Decades ago, the original method of animation was almost entirely by hand. That method has remained pretty much the same up until a few years ago. But even today with the aid of mechanical and electronic devices, the interplay of intellect, skill and creativity are still needed in order to produce a successful animation film.

With the advent of the newer technological aids, animation has also become highly departmentalized and at times extremely specialized in order to respond to the technical demands and time pressures of television, a major user of animation films.

But animation itself need not be as complicated as a television studio maze or a computer design. At the core, animation still relies on fundamental principles of motion and animation mechanics, a comprehension of camera effects and an appreciation of the broad potential of cinematography. Thus, the aim of this monograph is to show how smaller teams can make animated films, using very simple techniques and low-cost materials. With a grasp of these simplified fundamentals, anyone with drawing capability and an interest in media might start on his own animation project.

Characteristics of animation

Film animation[1] is a visual communication technique whose basic potential is to clarify the complex, to reveal the invisible, to teach quickly and concisely. It differs from *live-action filming* which as a rule takes pictures at a rate of twenty-four frames per second, though animation can incorporate live-action sequences into its production. But for the most part, animation utilizes the techniques of *stop-frame cinematography* whereby the camera is stopped after exposing single frames to allow the adjustments for the next frame's movements. Obviously, this method is a time-consuming one, requiring considerable manual labour and skill, not to speak of a sense of timing and motion.

Live-action and stop-frame cinematography each have their special potential to offer. In live-action cinematography with special high-speed cameras, one can expose several thousands of pictures in a single second, thus enabling the audience to study the trajectory of a bullet or the flight of a bird. One can also slow down the camera to take a picture once every hour and study the growth of a flower. In general, live-action filming conveys reality better than animation, since the photographic lens registers nature exactly as it is.

Animation, on the other hand, has its own characteristic way of stylizing nature, of clarifying and simplifying, and of breaking down events into understandable time segments. In order to better utilize the advantages of animation, it is helpful to describe in detail what animation can do.

1. All technical terms will be italicized when they are introduced. Readers can refer back to the first mention of a technical term by consulting the index on page 93.

It utilizes live action. Animation can incorporate live action, and break away from it, when the identification and added clarification given by live action are necessary.

The live-action picture has the obvious advantage of immediate authenticity. Here is a shot of an atomic pile; here is a railway signal box; here is a coal mine. But the complex surface of actuality has no real meaning unless the principles that make it function are demonstrated, as countless poorly made and superficially commentated documentaries (so-called documentaries) have shown. To move over from the actuality of the live-action picture into the purely analytical presentation of the animated drawing or diagram is to achieve the best of two worlds at once.

It illustrates through diagrams. Animation can superimpose a moving diagram upon the living image—a technique which both simplifies and analyses the working principles within.

Much of the plant, machinery or laboratory equipment used today is highly complex and needs considerable scientific or technological understanding to appreciate the processes and principles involved in their operation. According to the level of knowledge needed, animation presentation can be graded from the simplest, most basic form of demonstration to the fullest and most elaborate. This is a question of the animator adapting his particular skill in graphic demonstration to the requirements of the client or sponsor. Another point of some importance, especially in films on technical instruction, is that carefully designed animation films have proved themselves more easy to memorize than live-action films aiming to give comparable information.

It analyses processes and movements. The basic structure of the animation technique is the superimposition of transparent celluloid sheets, one over the other; each sheet or 'cel' bears only one moving section of the final composite moving image. In this way, the sectionalizing of a complex moving process (for example, a part of a machine or a stage in an industrial process) can be stripped down by peeling off layer after layer of the total image, so that the whole may be clearly seen as the sum of its parts.

This process is of great importance in clarifying a process or operation stages or phases. For example, one particular element can be isolated and fully treated, while other elements are kept in abeyance until their turn comes.

It simplifies through symbols. Animation can use a variety of graphic styles to illustrate the principles or processes involved. Styles can range from wholly imaginative or symbolic images to the merest, simplest diagrammatic representation, according to what is most appropriate. Apparently, aesthetic powers can enhance purely intellectual symbols.

This lifts animation from the level of a purely representational picture or diagram in motion to an artistic level, where the power of suggestion begins to operate and the imagination of the animator, as distinct from his craftmanship, is brought more fully into play. This can be particularly useful in industrial films intended for more general audiences, where demonstration of the nature of what is happening is more important than a detailed and accurate reconstruction process.

It emphasizes with colour. Included in the graphic style of animation are the advantages of colour. Colour can emphasize specific parts of an action to stress a point, thus avoiding prolonged verbal explanation. This is because colour differences can convey instantaneously what might well have to be laboriously pointed out in words alongside a purely black-and-white image. Colour can also be used symbolically in that kind of subject which allows psychological implications, or involves mood or feelings.

In live-action film, colour has seldom been used symbolically except occasionally in *avant-garde* production. In animation it is consistently used to assist an argument or create a mood.

It changes speed to illustrate. In contrast to live action, animation can more flexibly, more conveniently and with greater variety reduce or accelerate its speed in the presentation of a movement or a process. It is also economical, because important elements in a process may be presented in emphatic slow time, while the unimportant can be speeded up or merely flashed by.

This process is already familiar in live action, especially in scientific films using various accelerated speeds to show natural processes. In animation this technique can be extended to the demonstration of all forms of movement, particularly of machines, like a combustion engine.

It uses sound to stress action. Not only can comment (whether by word, by natural or artificial sound or by musical counterpoint) be synchronized with animation movements but timing the audio can be done with greater care and control than in live action, even to one-twenty-fourth of a second.

This is particularly helpful where the exact timing of rhythmic factors is essential. The emphatic, memorable use of natural or artificial sound and even music can also help to reinforce the image in numerous ways.

It plays on humour with cartoons. Cartoon film (the principal as well as the most flexible of the many branches of animation) is traditionally associated with humour, and a flash of humour here and there eases the concentration in any film on facts or information. It is, therefore, quite natural for the cartoon medium to relax and slip in a humorous comment or a comic symbol for effect.

In this regard, it is appropriate to ask whether the human figure in cartoons should be treated naturalistically or purposely aim at being comic or in the form of a caricature. The answer will depend on the nature of the film and on the attitude of both the sponsor and the animator to his intended audience. Actually, the more naturalistic the human figures are, the less natural they seem, for the cartoon is essentially an artificial medium that thrives on artificiality; if the need for a naturalistic figure is genuine, this implies that live action, not animation, is more appropriate for this particular film or sequence.

Human figures in cartoon can range from simplified drawings both designed and 'played' relatively straight, to grotesque ones made up of a few mobile lines. Some element of caricature is usually effective, and need by no means make its subject unsympathetic to an audience. It can in fact humanize him far more than any typed performance by a live actor in a poor quality live-action film.

These characteristics of animation have been adopted in many hundreds of films. This description of its potential is not the end of the line, it is the beginning. It is, however, essential to master the basic techniques before attempting to use one's imagination in an effective, constructive way. In animation, the old saying 'learn to walk before attempting to run' applies in a very real sense.

Chapter II

The range of animation techniques

Animation techniques can range from the simplest to the most complex. The choice of technique is guided by the consideration of informational objectives and the kind of impact the film is intended to make.

In general, it can be said that all animation techniques fall into two main categories: *flat animation* or *plastic animation.*

Flat animation is that performed on a two-dimensional surface, and usually necessitates the use of an animation rostrum. This category would include: the cel technique, cut-outs, collage, various kinds of moving diagrams, and even computer graphics and videograms. The fact that this kind of animation is done on a flat table or that it uses the flat surfaces of paper, celluloid, or a video screen does not rule out the possibility of achieving perspective, depth, and an illusion of three-dimensionality. Merely by the use of colours (light colours for far objects, dark colours for near objects), perspective lines (like two parallel rails receding gradually narrower into the distance), the size of objects relative to their nearness or distance, and so forth, the animator can create the

FIG. 1. *Cel technique. The pencil drawings are transferred on to celluloid sheets called cels, by tracing the lines in ink. With each cel held firmly on the artist's table by pegs similar to those on the animation rostrum, the artist can draw the graduated movements of a sequence. After this, the ink outlines are painted in colour. When all cels and background are finished, they are shot frame by frame on the animation rostrum. [Courtesy of Walt Disney.]*

FIG. 2. *Cel animation. At the rostrum, the animation cels and background are placed in position, held firm by the pegs at the upper edge of the table, and kept flat by the glass plate called a platen. The animator checks the dope sheet to assure exact execution of all details. [Courtesy of Halas & Batchelor Animation Ltd, London.]*

feeling of depth and plasticity even in what is technically flat animation.

Plastic animation is that which utilizes physical objects or figures. It exploits the plasticity, the form, the shape, the contour of the objects. Plastic animation can be of figures, such as puppets or marionettes or of objects, such as blocks, toy cars, or even models of molecules or galaxies.

In the discussion of the various animation techniques, it will become more evident how each can be used to convey certain messages or express particular feelings as required by the objectives of the film.

Flat animation

The cel technique

The *cel technique* is the most basic kind of flat animation. It utilizes a series of drawings made on plastic sheets, called *cels*. Animated figures or objects have individual cels drawn for each specific movement. An immobile background scene is drawn and painted on ordinary paper, and used throughout the scene. Both the animation cels and the background artwork are punched along one edge (top or bottom) to fit the standard pegs of the artist's table during the drawing stage and of the animation rostrum during the shooting. The use of separate cels for moving and non-moving objects is itself a measure of economy. The artist need sketch the static parts of a scene only once, thus concentrating his effort and time only on the moving objects or figures (see Figs. 1 and 2).

When preparing a background where a figure passes through an open door, the artist must prepare a background piece with an *overlay*. One sheet contains the background; the second (the overlay) contains only that part with the wall and the open door through which the figure will pass. The cel with the figure is then placed between the background sketch and the overlay, so that the figure will appear to pass through the door (where he should) and not through a solid wall (see Fig. 3).

FIG. 3. *Overlay. The wall marked 'Overlay' is a separate cel which allows figures to pass through the door without seeming to walk through the wall.*

Obviously, the cel technique requires a lot of man-hours and artistic effort. At the normal twenty-four frames per second, a 10-minute animation film could consume a maximum of 14,400 drawings, not counting backgrounds, overlays and cels for additionally animated figures or objects. But there are short cuts in both full animation (at least eight drawings per twenty-four frames) and limited animation (less than eight drawings per twenty-four frames).

Full animation

In actual practice, *full animation* (8 or more drawings per 24 frames) is applied mainly by professional studies using the technique of cel animation. The flexibility of such animation allows the widest possible expression. It is a very expensive practice and as a rule only advertising agencies can afford to pay for it. We have already referred to the fact full animation consists of preparing eight or more individual drawings in each second of time unit or for every twenty-four frames. This formula is not to be taken literally, since no animation should be planned in such a regular way, not even full animation.

When a character hops along in double-frame animation (two exposures for each drawing), each hopping cycle of 1 second duration would use up twelve drawings. But at the point where the figure touches the ground, a squash would be needed and this would consume two additional hold frames. In this case the rhythm of the cycle would be as follows: 1/2/3/4 (plus two holding frames for anticipation or squash-reaction), 5/6, 7/8, 9/10, 11/12, 13/14, 15/16, 17/18, 19/20, 21/22 (end hop and return to the first frame).

In this case only ten drawings are required in the cycle. But rarely is only one figure used in a scene; and naturally, the more figures that are featured, the more animation has to be produced.

It is essential, however, that single animation (only one exposure for each drawing or twenty-four drawings per second) should be used in quick motions like body turns, fights and runs, whether quick or slow. Single animation should also be used in close ups, facial expressions, or hand movements where large changes of the body movement from one frame to another can cause an unpleasant jitter. Although mouth movement can be simplified to match voices, smooth animation demands synchronization of sound to lip movement in each frame, since the changes of words occur at single frame speed.

The greatest care should be applied with repeat cycle animation and panoramic background movement. It is essential that the distance of movement travelled in a repeat cycle (the hop for example) should be compensated for in the speed and distance of panning movement of the background in the opposite direction. If the two are 'out of step', the animation will appear to be sliding backwards or forwards. Similarly, the ground distance covered by walks in one direction should be the same as that covered by background panning in the other direction.

Limited animation

Paradoxically, greater skill is required for *limited animation* than for full animation. In fact, one should work first on full animation in order to understand what can be omitted in a movement. It should also be realized that in limited animation, the number of *key animations* is proportionately increased, since it is the in-between frames which are usually left out in the process of production. Consequently, the audience will see the keys longer on the screen, and the quality of these drawings needs to be better.

On the average, limited animation utilizes six animated drawings for each second of screen time. With careful planning and special skill the average could be reduced to four per second (see Fig. 4). But one must not come to the conclusion that in every scene of 10 seconds, one should produce exactly sixty or forty drawings. This 'average' is based on the total number of drawings produced in the whole

Fig. 4. *Limited animation, when used skilfully, can be done with only four cels per second, each frame receiving six exposures. Note the use of swish lines to smooth out the movement.*

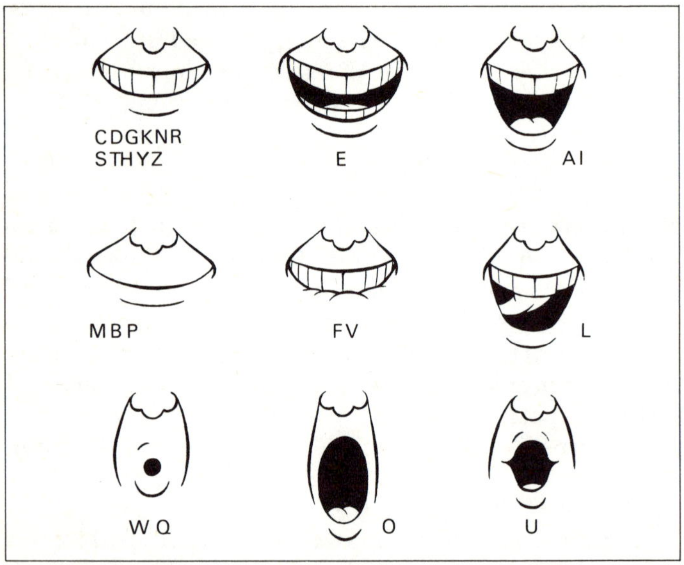

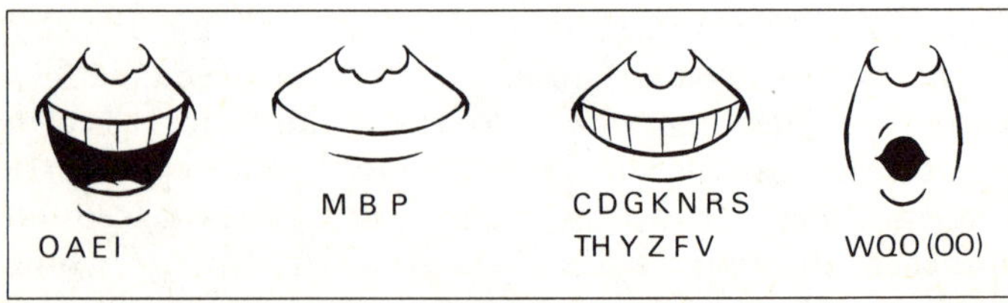

Fig. 5. *Animating mouth movements. The nine basic positions (above) which, with skill, can be reduced to four (below).*

production and includes all the possible repeat cycles and held positions. It can happen that one scene requires only twelve drawings, but another may need over a hundred. The greater the number of repeat animations, the less drawings are used. Calculating the repeats can save time and work.

Similar liberties can be taken with the animation of dialogue. Basically nine mouth positions can combine all the synchronization points for the alphabet (see Fig. 5 showing the nine animated positions for oral sounds; with an idea how these positions can be reduced to four).

The animator can utilize more or less mouth positions, as required by the nature of the film. For sophisticated animation on a large cinema screen, practically all words need different drawings. For quickly produced television films, it is possible to use only four positions. Since the television has a small screen one can afford such liberties, provided the mouth positions are expertly manipulated. The camera can also contribute to the reduction of drawings by dissolving from one position to another. This device, if used intelligently and interspersed with animation, can give the illusion of movement with only a few drawings. But to achieve a flow of motion, it is advisable to maintain a minimum of eight frames.

The camera can also contribute to limited animation by its capability of tracking. A complex shape, like the Concorde aeroplane (provided it is photographed against a neutral background) can be made to appear to move by having the camera track in or out of it.

In brief, limited animation using the cel technique, can be produced quite easily and simply. Try to keep to the following guidelines to save time and work and still maintain an artistic animation:

1. Simplify movements.
2. Avoid perspective (three dimensionality) as much as possible in any character or object to be animated.

FIG. 6. *Cut-out animation can be made very simply, using coloured paper and scissors. A greater precision in timing and movement is needed to make the cut-outs move smoothly and effectively. [Courtesy of VEB Defa Studio für Trickfilme, Dresden.]*

3. Use backgrounds to replace animation by background panning.
4. Maximize the use of camera performance, by dissolves, tracking or other camera movements.
5. Finally, make a few drawings do the work of many, by knowing for how many frames a drawing can be held, and how many times one animation cycle can be repeated.

With the help of these guidelines and an ample use of imagination, limited animation can save time and labour, without a conspicuous revelation of it, but quality of production must never be sacrificed by drastic reductions of drawings and backgrounds. It is for this reason that it is advisable to plan for limited animation at the scripting stage, before starting the production.

Other forms of flat animation

Cut-out animation. Another simple technique is *cut-out animation*—with cut-out characters and objects. The required figures are designed, cut out, placed on their proper background and manipulated by hand under the rostrum camera. A further development of this method is to use a magnetized board with magnets glued to the backs of the cut-outs. The added advantage of magnetic cut-outs is that they keep their position better and one can even manipulate the objects vertically, while with paper cut-outs it is essential to maintain a horizontal position in order to avoid displacement (see Fig. 6).

A cut-out character usually consists of seven different parts. The head, neck, body, two arms, two legs. It can be far more complex if desired or needed. An object like a tractor may simply need only three parts: the main body of the machine and two wheels. Complexity depends on the tasks to be performed.

Animated cut-outs can be assembled with paper or with thin magnetized metal sheets. If paper is to be used, it should be thick enough not to curl under the heat of the lights and to allow easy assembly of the various sections of the character or object. If metal is used, it must be thin enough so that a nylon or metal thread and needle can go through it for joining the parts together.

Once the characters and objects are designed and coloured, the separate parts should be joined together with the help of thread and needle. The joints should be camouflaged with self colours or, even better, invisibly patched by gluing another layer of paper or metal of the same colour to cover the joints.

After assembling the cut-outs, it is important to assure that they can be easily manipulated under the camera and will stay put firmly in between every single adjustment for animation. If they spring back, the thread which keeps them together should be loosened up, until the positions can be manipulated safely.

Cut-out animation can provide for expressions on the characters' faces, as well as animation in perspective, despite the fact that the approach provides basically a two-dimensional appearance. For facial expressions, one may use separate eyes with various facial looks or just eyeballs moving within the shape of the eye itself. These positions must be adjusted under the camera according to the type of mood required by the script. For animating the objects in perspective one is obliged to cut-out each position separately. For instance, a horse turning from one side to another would require at least twelve phases of cut-out figures, each one placed in determined positions until the full turn around is achieved.

It is advisable to use simply designed backgrounds under the cut-out shapes without extra layers so that the cut-outs can be manipulated without collision. It is also advisable to use as few cut-outs at one time as possible in order to avoid overlapping the characters.

Naturally, great concentration is essential to animate cut-outs under the camera since it requires an element of improvisation as far as timing is concerned and an instinct for what can be achieved with such basic tools. For this reason, it is advisable to obtain help to operate the camera. If a cameraman carries out the photography, controls the lighting and the exposure, then the cut-out animator is able to focus full attention on the manipulation of the scene, the timing, and the many other little details which always occur during the shooting.

Scratchback. The technique of *scratchback* is a simple way of expressing growth of any sort. A single drawing is made, containing the whole development of the visual information. The animator can achieve a continuous, smooth movement by scratching off or erasing the drawing stage by stage between camera exposures, while the film is run in reverse. Projecting the film forward creates the illusion of the diagram being assembled in all its stages up to its full extent. Scratchback is particularly useful for graphs, words that write themselves, and drawings that express growth.

Diagrams with live action. By combining animation with live action, it is possible to compare the living image with the moving diagram which simplifies its shape and analyses the forces which move it. The combination can be effected most simply by cutting between live action and animation. These cuts are most effective when the animation is designed from an actual frame of the live-action scene. Animation and live film can also be combined in the same scene.

Aside from clarifying live-action processes, the animated diagram can also be used to simplify, analyse and express other visible processes which would ordinarily be inaccessible or even unclear when using live-action photography. Its fullest capability, however, is in the presentation of processes which cannot even be perceived in actuality, such as the forces of magnetism, gravity and electricity; the action of physical laws; and the pattern of microscopic or cosmic events. Time can be expanded or contracted; events of a few milliseconds can be shown at length. The transformation of decayed animal organisms into oil, a process of nature requiring several millions of

FIG. 7. *Plastic animation exploits the form, shape and contour of objects. Moving parts must be firmly attached, but allow free movement. [Courtesy of George Pal Productions Inc., Hollywood.]*

FIG. 8. *An example of clarifying scientific concepts through animation from* A is for Atom, *a film for General Electric by J. Sutherland, Hollywood.*

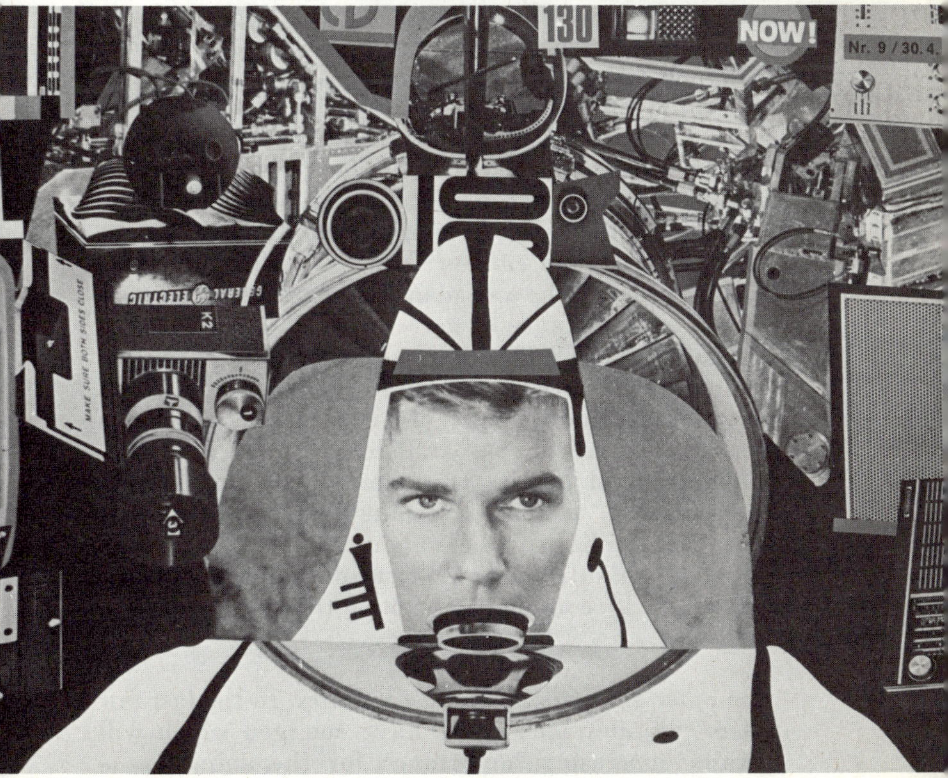

FIG. 9. *Collage animation combines both graphic and photographic materials under the rostrum camera. The materials are placed and shot in a sequence that drives home a visual message.*

years, can be shown in a few minutes. Important elements in a process can be emphatically slowed down or speeded up to show the underlying patterns involved (see Fig. 8).

Collage animation. One usually refers to *collage animation* as a technique of improvisation under the rostrum camera. In this approach practically any visual material would do: cut-outs from newspapers, photographs, drawings, lettering or the combination of all. The various materials are assembled under the camera, and pasted into a fixed position as one goes along. The pictures are progressively exposed as they gradually assume a concise shape, configuration or graphic message (see Fig. 9).

There are occasions when the mixture of the different visual elements may be quite interesting, but could also look filmically inorganic and graphically disorganized. To avoid this pitfall, the animator should make sure that the various visual elements blend well. Photographs should show some visual relation to the other graphic elements. The improvised animation of cut-out shapes and the stop-frame shooting should be pre-planned in terms of frames, seconds and distance of movements.

This form of animation can be quite inexpensive, yet extremely artistic. The basic disadvantage of this technique is the difficulty of sustaining interest for a period of time. Shapes and designs that jump too violently tend to tire the eyes quickly or distract unnecessarily thereby lessening the impact of the film. Some relief can be sought in the use of cross-dissolves to introduce new cut-out objects on the screen, or in combination with other forms of animation.

Computer animation and videographics. In the last few years two new techniques have emerged which will assume increasing importance for the animator as their cost decreases or their accessibility becomes liberal: computer animation and videographics. Both depend on complex electronic machine intelligence and could be very expensive if not used in the right context. So far, the main use of *computer animation* has been confined to animate geometrical shapes which it can do with extreme mathematical precision. It can also carry out animation in perspective, but such a performance is even more complex.

Videographics is an electronic device used in television studios to produce at high speed title designs, announcements, credits and other information. When patched in to a television mixing console, this video information can be combined with other television material by electronic keying, fades or wipes. But since most individual animators do not have access to this equipment, specific techniques are not discussed in depth in this monograph.

Plastic animation

When speaking of plastic animation, one usually refers to animation with three-dimensional figures, like puppets and marionettes. From our point of view, we would like to enlarge upon this definition and include objects of a wider range like molecules and atoms which are often needed in scientific instruction, or models of machines which could be advantageously used in industrial training films. We thus distinguish two types of plastic animation: *figure animation* using puppets; and *non-figure animation* which covers any other type of object. In every case, it is the plastic appearance of the object which justifies the choice of this approach.

The difference between flat and plastic animation lies in two basic factors: first in the appearance; second, in the method of execution. In the cel or cut-out animation, appearance is graphic; movement takes place in the two-dimensional world even if the figures occasionally give an illusion of moving in three dimensions; the models are rounded but only look plastic. In the animation of figures or objects, plasticity is one of the major visual appeals and should be the most important aspect to strive for.

It should be capable of creating a world of its own, totally different from any other form of animation, providing tricks which only stop-motion photography with three-dimensional objects could do. But this medium is not quite as flexible as flat animation, since quick changes in a world of three dimensions are more difficult to manipulate and visually absorb.

The methods of plastic and flat animation also differ. Plastic animation can be photographed with the camera at an angle of varying degree between 15 and 45 per cent; it need not be filmed at a fixed angle of 90 per cent. The camera is usually fixed on a movable tripod, and not mounted on a rostrum. The shooting technique and lighting, therefore, more closely resemble live-action photography. Camera moves should be arranged on tracking rails fixed to the ground, and the angle of the camera adjusted during each stop. Each adjustment must be carried out manually on the objects in between camera exposures, and the animator should know the exact degree of each adjustment. This is often a question of guesswork, although most model animators can develop a quick sense of timing. Complex magnetic control can be installed but is very expensive.

Shooting plastic animation

The frame-by-frame changes in the aspect of the objects can be made in the following ways:

1. Modification of lighting and exposure.
2. Shifting the position of the camera or the objects.
3. Movement of articulated objects.
4. Substitution of objects. This last method is the most difficult and the costliest, but the most versatile of the four.

In each case, strict rigidity of the objects during exposure and high precision in their movement are necessary. The phases of movement are calculated and numbered in advance on what is known as a score. Test negatives are made and screened for rhythm control and, if necessary, the score is modified before the final shooting, which takes much less time than its preparation.

When animating models, full concentration is essential since the performance includes several steps of operation: handling the objects by moving limbs, heads, eyes or the whole model itself; controlling the camera, lighting and exposure; and a sense of timing throughout. Here, more than in any other type of animation, it is most advisable to co-operate with a cameraman who is responsible for the lighting and the whole of the camera operation.

Choice of materials

Today there is a great deal of diverse material available to construct three-dimensional objects, depending on whether soft or hard, stiff or bendable material is required. For figure animation, rubber or plastic material is often used with an interior wire frame to hold the figure's head and limbs in position.

Another useful material for model making is soft wood. It also has the advantage of taking paint, which in case of puppet animation saves dressing a a character. One can also combine the materials and use soft wood for the body and head, and wires for the limbs of a puppet. Wires of all sorts and shapes, including ordinary pipe-cleaning wire, are very useful as they easily bend and stay in position. The newest material, however, which has spread round the world as the most useful tool for plastic animation is plasticine itself. Previously, due to its softness, it melted under the rostrum lights and was found unsuitable for animation. During recent years, a much harder version has been marketed which stays firm, sculptures easily, and is pliable for changing movements as one goes along. The wide range of colours adds to its flexibility and manœuvrability.

The choice of material is vitally important in model animation. Soft materials should be avoided since they are difficult to control and hold in the same position from one frame to the next. Model materials should be firm but mouldable, and capable of maintaining a frozen position during stop-frame exposures. Some samples are: sand, which can be shifted easily under the camera; stones, which can be moved from frame to frame; hard paper, which can be bent and forced to stay put; match sticks, which can be marched along and cheap to buy; even glass, which can be moulded under heat.

In figure animation, the question of dressing the puppet is usually as difficult as its manipulation. Dressing in soft cloth often obstructs free animation as the cloth is liable to move or waft during exposure. It is advisable to paint the cloth to stiffen it. The features of the face should also be painted, unless mouth animation or eye movement is called for. In this case, both these parts have to be attached to the face and animated separately from the body.

Fixing these parts to the face as well as fixing the head on to the body calls for a touch of engineering skill. There are several ways of doing this, depending on the material being used. The important factor here is that no animation should start without making sure that each part of the body can be operated under the camera frame by frame.

The potential of plastic animation is still to be explored. It certainly has an important contribution to make in instructional and educational films.

These then are the main techniques of animation. Each can be used separately for an entire animation film or can be combined with other animation techniques or even with live sequences. The selection of technique or techniques depends on the objectives of the film and the kind of audience intended, as expressed in the treatment.

For all these techniques, it is essential to understand what each can do and express and the kind of work involved so as not to burden the production team unnecessarily. Animation work undoubtedly is laborious and time-consuming. But as shown above, reasonable economy can be had with an astute management of resources, talents and work scheduling.

Chapter III

Animation mechanics

The essence of animation is to create movement through the sequenced exposure of individual drawings. There are certain essential laws and physical principles attached to this practice, which the most basic and primitive animation cannot ignore without risking bitter failure and long, time-consuming activity.

Sympathetic movement

The first principle is to understand the difference between the *sympathetic* and *unsympathetic movement* (see Fig. 10). In animation there are certain limits which the eyes can accept as continuous movement. When a live-action camera swings across the horizon and photographs a tree in the foreground, one obtains automatically a three-dimensional image with a background receding naturally into the distance. If a car moves across the screen, it introduces a secondary movement. The camera lens would blur the shape of the car as it moves across the screen, but all would appear to be natural. Such a camera movement may appear to jitter slightly, but would be appreciated as a clever shot. But if such an action were to be animated, it would look wrong. The shape of the tree in the foreground and the car in the mid-distance would look too hard in an animated sequence. Due to the hard shape of the objects and simplified background, it would acquire an 'optical jitter' causing what is generally known as an unsympathetic movement. Such a movement must be specially treated by designing the objects with softer outlines. And, if the motion is quick, the artist must draw the shapes with a blurred image to avoid the optical jitter which is otherwise known as the *stratoscopic optical interference* (the illusion of multiple-imaging of an object in motion).

In animation, one is obliged to persuade the eyes and the brain to accept the animated interpretation of a natural movement and make it look as natural as the real thing. In fact, if one has more control over the various elements which make up such a scene, one is able to achieve an illusion of reality greater than that of the actual live-action camera. In order to achieve such an objective, one is obliged to use softer shapes which avoid the illusion of jitter and create movements which are as much as possible sympathetic to the eyes.

To achieve sympathetic movement, four factors have to be considered: the shape of an object; the distance between each movement; the dynamics of the movement; the timing of the movement.

Shape

The avoidance of square shapes is advisable in animation. The round appearance of so many well-known cartoon characters is not entirely accidental. From the animation point of view these characters are made up of functional shapes combining the values and the basis of sympathetic movement and the manœuvrability of repeatable animation. There are occasions, however, when in diagrammatic ani-

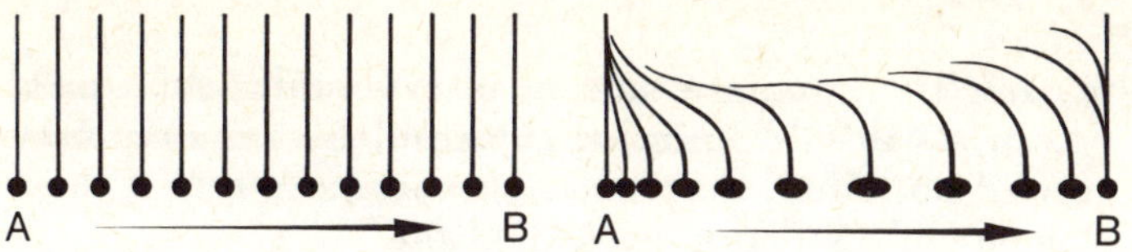

FIG. 10. *Sympathetic movement. The upper set of lines shows unsympathetic movement whereby the in-between animations are placed at equal distances from each other and each figure is exactly the same as the preceding one. Such an animation would show stratoscopic optical interference. To achieve sympathetic movement, the distance between the centre animations is wider than at the extremes. To show the direction and effect of movement, the line is streamlined and the ball is elongated, as the figure moves to the centre; they return to normal at the end of the motion.*

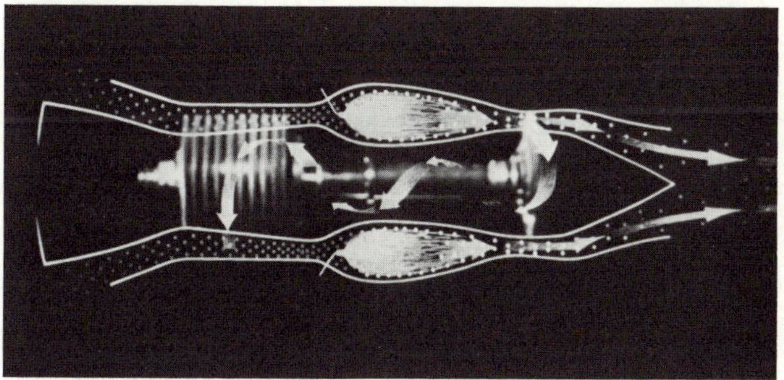

FIG. 11. *Live-action filming can be combined with animation diagrams to clarify processes or mechanisms. Here, a turbine casing is diagrammatically superimposed on a 'live' shaft to illustrate the flow of air around the turbine blades. [Country of Shell Films, United Kingdom.]*

FIG. 12. *Norman McLaren, a pioneer in film animation, prepares artwork for a film on mathematics. [Courtesy of National Film Board of Canada.]*

mation the square shape is unavoidable, such as a box or a valise. Animating these objects requires very careful handling. Softened edges in motion and some element of distortion are called for.

Distance

The distance between movements from one frame to another is of prime importance in the skill of animation.

There are a great number of factors to consider in dealing with this problem. In general, the larger the distance in movement between each drawing the quicker is the movement. For slower movement, more drawings with smaller distances in movement are necessary. There are, however, limits at both ends of the scale. Let us take the example of 16-mm film which passes the projector lens at the speed of twenty-four frames per second. If we used only six drawings per second to depict an object moving across the screen, the movement would appear to be blurred and stroboscopic. Jitter and unsympathetic movement would be obvious. If we used twelve drawings per second, a figure passing from one end of the frame would appear quite normal without any distortion whatsoever and no problem with strobing or blur would occur.

For fast action, it is advisable to introduce some form of shading lines into the fast moving forms. These are generally known as speed lines or swish lines. These forms should continue the path of the movement of the object in the preceding drawing unless for an exaggerated effect; the movement needs to be overemphasized. In many animated productions, the object itself is replaced by speedlines, but this conversion can only work when the high speed of the action requires it. As soon as the action decreases it is advisable to gradually reintroduce the actual design of the object again until the motion stops and the object regains its normal form.

As with so many other theories in animation, these guidelines on distance should be applied with intelligence, and not as hard rules since every case may be a totally different animation problem like the flight of jet planes, the migration of ants, or the life cycle of frogs.

Dynamics of movement

All movements are subject to certain principles of gravity which determine their behaviour. These principles apply to live photography just as much as animation, and their roots exist in real life. Although we do not have to study physical science in detail, it is useful to know the basic *dynamics of motion*, since animation has to re-create this physical condition. Newton, the British scientist, observed that if an object is still, it tends to remain still (law of inertia). If an object is in motion, it tends to remain in motion (law of momentum).

He further observed that the state of stillness and motion can be changed only by an outside force and that the body will move in a direct line in which the force is applied, until another force acts to change its direction. And further, he demonstrated that every action causes an equal reaction in the opposite direction.

The tendency to remain still may be classified as 'inertia', and the tendency to continue the movement, 'momentum'. Inertia and momentum, and the related concept of 'gravity' are extremely relevant in the planning of any movement. In real life, these forces condition the behaviour of all objects. A live action camera as a rule merely records the behaviour of moving shapes, but animation has to re-create them manually which, though extremely labour-consuming, enables the animator to control, to manipulate, to adapt movement at his will. If the animated film calls for it, one may exaggerate momentum and inertia, but by doing so one must never forget the basic natural laws which govern the behaviour of movement. All starting points must be based on the true dynamics of motion and all exaggeration must be done with a specific purpose in mind. Otherwise, such motion will appear to be false. Animation can

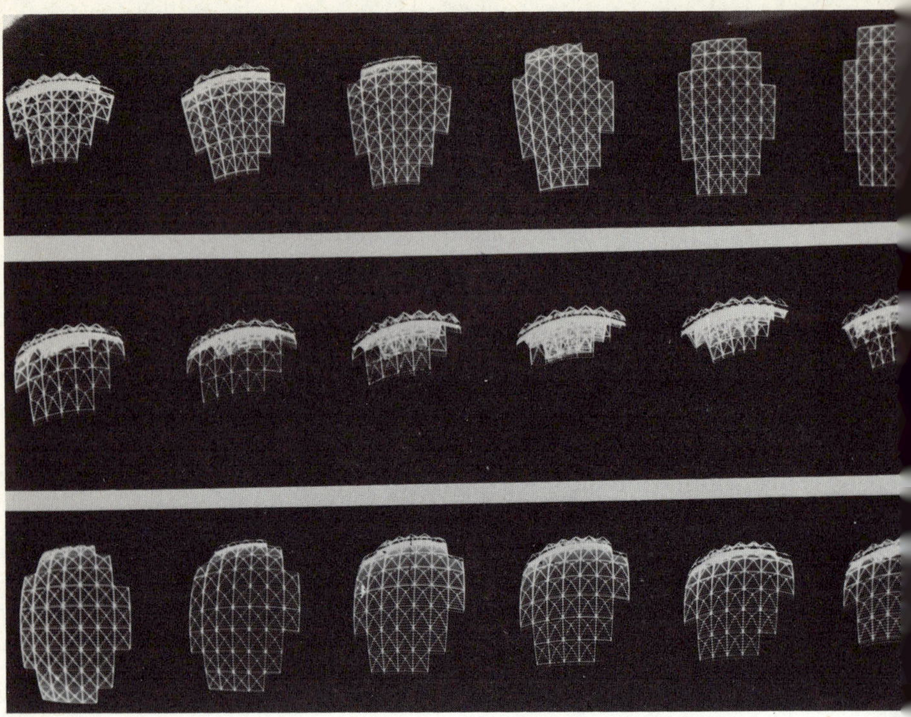

FIG. 13. *Computer animation of radar is filmed for* contact, *a story on electricity for CGE France, by John Halas and Joy Batchelor. [Courtesy of Educational Film Centre Ltd, London.]*

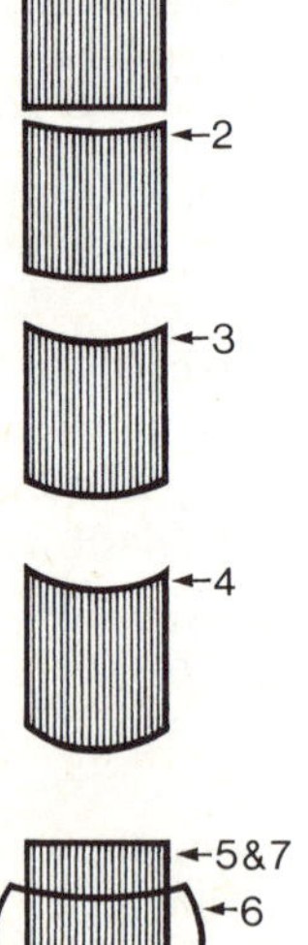

FIG. 14. *Squash. When a square object is falling, it gradually assumes a streamlined shape in the direction of the fall. Upon being stopped, as when a box hits the pavement, the square shape will be squashed slightly before resuming its normal square shape. The sequence from 1 to 7 shows how this would be done in animation to produce sympathetic movement.*

even defy gravity and give the illusion of liberating an animated character from the forces of gravity —and this is their chief appeal. But before attempting to manipulate these elements, it is necessary to understand beforehand how they behave under normal physical conditions.

In preparing for animation, one also has to deal with a great number of other factors: the particular behaviour of the character; its weight or mass; the material it is made of; its outward appearance; and how all these factors influence its movement.

The weight of an object is an important consideration in determining speed of action. As Newton observed, a heavy object is harder to start up than a lighter one, but once in motion it has greater inertia of movement and is more difficult to stop. When it collides with another object, its impetus is greater since it is more reluctant to stop. The object will tend to move in the direct line in which the external force is applied until collision stops it or another force changes its direction.

In all motion, animation has to deal with these various factors of size, shape, weight and material with just the right amount of distortion and squash. In the three basic stages of animation dynamics ('anticipation', the preparation for the movement; 'action', the actual movement; and 'reaction', the completion of it), one must always search for the best way to convey motion. A precise understanding of motion dynamics as well as experience in relating character behaviour to weight, material and shape will lead to animate movement with just the right amount of distortion and squash, thus producing consistently sympathetic movement (see Fig. 14).

Timing

Timing is a skill of its own, just as much as the gift of drawing or design. Its importance should never be underrated, as it is one of the elements where the handmade method of animated film gives full flexibility and total control.

Time is a basic condition of life itself. We are born, live and die; we experience a beginning, a middle and an end. Film is conditioned much the same way, it has a beginning, a middle and a finish. What to put into it can often be considered from the point of view of timing. Each second of the film has to be filled with some aspect of happening and its value depends on how creatively the film is conceived and executed. The result can be made amusing or instructive. One can achieve impossible tricks or put across some valuable points. The film-maker can speed up a whole geological period into a few seconds or slow down the motion of a bullet and study its motion for minutes. Solely by the skilled use of timing, he can establish a hushed mood by choosing a slow rhythmic beat, induce excitement by speeding up an action, or spark humour by making a figure walk at an unnatural speed.

In timing an animated action, one should realize from the start that it is a fallacy to copy the timing and behaviour of real people and objects. Such an animation would appear too slow and would risk failure by following reality slavishly. One should utilize real movement only as a starting point in order to create an animated movement proper to the character or object. Since animated objects or figures are simplified, they represent only symbols of reality. Their behaviour can thus be observed more quickly than that of live objects. This is why they usually tend to demand quicker speed.

Speed frame ratio

The speed of animation is in direct relation to the number of frames it occupies on the film as well as to the speed of projection. The more frames a movement lasts, the slower it will appear on the screen. Conversely, the fewer the frames, the faster the movement.

The normal speed of the sound track is standardized at twenty-four frames per second for cinema and non-theatrical screenings and at twenty-five frames per second for television. By and large, most animation timing is carried out at twenty-four frames per second. This gives a conveniently scaled relationship of the number of frames to the parts of a second, as follows:

1 frame	= 1/24 sec.	8 frames	= 1/3 sec.
2 frames	= 1/12 sec.	12 frames	= 1/2 sec.
3 frames	= 1/8 sec.	16 frames	= 2/3 sec.
4 frames	= 1/6 sec.	18 frames	= 3/4 sec.
6 frames	= 1/4 sec.	24 frames	= 1 sec.

Even if a film is silent and consequently projected at the normal silent speed of eighteen frames a second, it is still better to base all timing on sound speed since its conversion is simpler and provides a wider range of possibilities for movement.

Before any animation work is begun, the animator must decide on the over-all timing of the film and often of each scene in the film. It occurs frequently that the very speed and character of the sound track predetermine the density of animation change. For this reason the sound track itself has to be analysed in terms of the number of film frames per spoken syllabus or beat of music. A sense of timing developed from both sharp instinct and experience is essential for this work. A stopwatch that reads in fractions of seconds is a useful tool. The action that takes place within time fractions should be indicated on a sound chart by the animator.

Timing, distance, size, speed

In timing a movement, the speed of an object must always be determined in relation to its size in the frame, its position in the frame, its relationship with other objects in the scene and the movement it has to perform. When watching a moving object on the cinema screen, the apparent speed may not be the same as the actual speed it tries to convey. For example, a jet-plane moving across the screen at a height of 10,000 metres, would seem to move much slower than one at 1,000 metres, although the actual speed of both may be the same.

If two objects of the same size are advancing at the same speed but at different distances from the lens, the one nearer to the camera would appear to cross the screen in less time even if the proportion of the length which they advance for every single frame is the same. On the other hand, if two objects of different proportion are moving at the same speed, the proportion of their own length advanced for every frame will be different.

The size of the object in relation to the distance covered in the frame determines the degree and the extent of distortion required. The jet in the distance travelling at an enormous speed would require some distortion and speed lines, but the nearer one to the camera would need none at all. Any form of machinery animating across the screen in the foreground, then re-entering again the screen in the middle distance, should move the same proportion of its length per frame in each size, if it is to appear to maintain the same speed.

Should a smaller object follow a larger one, but move at the same speed as the larger one, it would require some form of distortion and speedlines as its apparent speed-length compared to distance moved is greater.

A further help to achieve sympathetic and smooth movement is to animate an object beaming into the curve line it is following. For example, a rectangle shape moving along a straight line should remain rectangular; but if it moves along a curved line, its shape should be streamlined along the curve of movements, provided the object is animating at a sufficient speed to be distorted at all.

In animation, many alternatives are possible even with the simplest walk cycle or flight of objects. Each problem has to be solved on its own merit and according to the creative ability of the film-maker. To take an example, a walk in a twelve-frame cycle is numbered as 1 and 13 on the animated drawings, as the figure moves his leg from one extreme position to another before repeating. This set of drawings may give the right speed, but the movement may be too slow, or too quick, or too flat; or the legs may not be lifted high enough; or the whole action may lack rhythm, style or character. In timing complex movements, one often is obliged to test them not only for the right speed but also for the desired effect. In small budget films, this may not always be possible and reluctantly one is forced to accept the first take of the scene. Obviously, a right sense of timing can save time and cost in production.

Should a film have the advantages of pre-recorded music, the beats of the sound-track not only provide a helpful indication of time progression, but also a natural link between the rhythm of the beat and the rhythm of the movement. Such relationships between sound and image have been well exploited in animation and there is no reason why maximum use should not be made of it. If there is no music, one can still make use of an underlying rhythm in the movement itself to make decisions in timing. For such imaginary rhythm, the subdivision of twenty-four frames (1 second) may be the most convenient definition. Two beats in a second would provide twelve frames per movement, three beats eight frames, four beats six frames. For irregular movements where the key positions are estimated to occur at frame intervals of say six, three, four, eight this approach is just as valuable.

A developed sense of timing can lead to economy of work when the animator knows which animated positions can be held for a certain number of frames. Even the most experienced studios animate in double frames, that is, two exposures per drawing or twelve drawings per second (except for very quick turns). It is also quite conceivable to animate in three frames (each drawing receives three exposures) and still retain an illusion of fluidity. But the animator must know exactly at what shot size and at what position he is able to take such liberties, otherwise the animation will appear jerky and disturbing.

It is the key animator's responsibility to analyse the movements and specify the key drawings (for new movements) and the in-between drawings (for repeat cycles). Although animation art can be laborious and time-consuming, a developed sense of timing can help immensely to economize on time and work.

Chapter IV

Pre-production of animation

Even the simplest type of film has to go through an essential planning process which determines the step-by-step stages of production. The preparation for this is not unlike the work of an architect building a house. The form, the size, the stages and the material have to be pre-arranged before the actual work can start, and a time-table drawn up for it once such information is available. In the production of a simple film, the film-maker will very likely take the place of both the architect and the builder.

From the first, it is essential to be satisfied that the subject matter is suitable for the medium of animation. If the subject lends itself to be made in live action or it is more suitable for film-strip production, one should not use animation at all. For guidance on the suitability of animation, one may refer to the points listed in the previous chapter.

This done, the film-maker should clearly define the objective of the film and base his material on adequate research. If a film is to convey facts, the facts must be right. If it is to be based on a debate putting forward several points of view, the content

IDEA
Storyboard
SOUND
PICTURE
Music
Design &
Animation
Voices
& Effects
Tracing
& Painting
Recording
Background
Dubbing
Camera
Editing
FINISHED
FILM

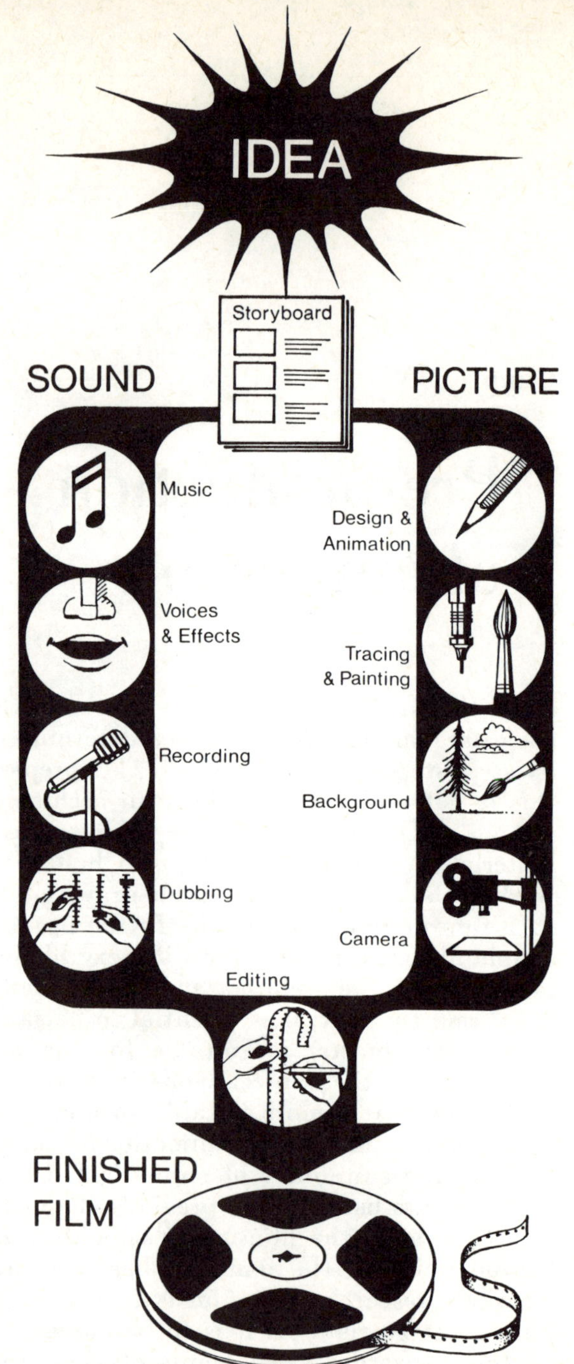

Fig. 15.

must be authentic. If the film is intended to be a demonstration film showing how to carry out an operation it must be based on logical, sequential order, and must be accurate.

In any case, the structure of the film must be simple and clear, showing a natural progression in time and a carefully planned build-up aimed at achieving the objective of the film.

The film-maker should seek to accommodate the intelligence of the audience, neither going too far above their technical or scientific comprehension nor underestimating their capabilities.

Treatment

In order to get these factors in proper perspective, it is helpful to prepare a written *treatment* of the project.

This treatment, consisting of 500 to 1,000 words, states the developments and changes in the film and what part the various characters, if any, will play in it. It also indicates such basic elements as humour (if it helps the story), length, rough continuity development, the type of graphic design, or the type of technique employed, i.e. cut-outs, cel animation, combined techniques or special effects. The ideas should be stated concisely in the form of descriptive sentences. It has to be remembered that a film treatment is not a literary work on its own merit, but a means of description on how the film should be treated. If the subject matter is complex and requires scientific advice and authentification by technical experts, it is not unusual for the preparation of the treatment to last almost as long as the production of the film itself.

A sample treatment (Scene 9)

	Cartoon	*Commentary*
V.	The salesman character enters through the door, led by the client. The client closes the door behind him.	
		[Murmuring voices which die down as soon as the salesman has entered the room and the door has closed behind him]
	Quick close-up of the salesman's face whose eyes are like large terrified marbles.	
		If everything has gone well up to now, then the next stage is usually: the living-room.
VI.	Shot in the opposite direction: grouped as though for a family photograph, four or five figures look at the entering salesman curiously (children, wife, grandfather, female or male neighbour). Camera tracks towards the group until only rolling eyes can be seen.	And there can be many surprises awaiting the salesman here. Frequently he will not be alone with the client. Therefore, he must always be prepared to deal with several interlocutors at the same time. He must learn to determine correctly their significance for the conversation.
VII.	The salesman takes a few hesitant uncertain steps into the room. He treads on a large ball of wool which is in front of his feet, trips and gets hopelessly entangled in it.	*[The silence is broken only by timid steps and suppressed giggling]* Otherwise there are many tripwires in close succession here. For a simple reason.
VIII.	Heads of the group, which break into infernal laughter.	*[Thunderous fall, then an explosion of fiendish laughter]*

Storyboard

Once the treatment is approved, the *storyboard* can be started. In the form of rough sketches, the visual aspect of the film with its graphic style is evolved. The choice of the most appropriate approach will vary immensely for different purposes. It may be realistic like a photographic object: or if the concept requires it, one may use a totally symbolistic graphic design. No matter what the subject is, the storyboard should have an attractive appearance and clearly show the progression of the film step by step.

A storyboard usually takes the form of a series of visual sketches like a series of strips, with pictures showing the action and captions describing it. If sound is required either in the form of effects, dialogue or commentary, these elements should be described and developed together with the visual aspect. For each minute of film (60 seconds of time unit), it is advisable to produce fifty to sixty pictures, each approximately 9×12 cm in size. Even in a rough storyboard, colour could help clarify some factual points or, if the film has a story continuity, accentuate the dramatic development. The storyboard also indicates the choreography of the film and the duration of each scene.

Design

It is important at the outset to realize that there is a substantial difference between making a single static picture and producing a film, even though it is composed of a series of 'static' pictures.

The onlooker can take time over a newspaper cartoon or a poster design displayed in the street. He can linger over an illustration or a painting at a gallery, as long as his interest holds. But in a film, the drawings pass at a great succession of speed, and their comprehension is strongly influenced by the composite effect of the speed at which they appear, their movement, the changing story development, and the nature of the background textures.

In creating a single, static picture, the ordinary artist can utilize a comparatively liberal attitude towards textures, colours and shapes. But the animator is restricted in his option because the drawings have to be reproduced a great number of times and are subjected to certain optical distortions which must be compensated for, in order to achieve good results on the screen. In designing static objects, the artist must have graphic skill. When designing objects that move, the animator must have a degree of acting capability as well.

In animation films, whether the objects are 'real' (cars, aeroplanes, ships), 'diagrammatic' (drawings of molecules or microbes), 'abstract' (mathematical equations or directional signs) or 'imaginary' (cartoon characters), three basic rules have to be adopted:

1. Simplicity of shapes for easy recognition.
2. Designs which can be easily manipulated in every possible position in space.
3. Structures which can be drawn with easy speed in case a great number of phases are to be animated.

All designs, no matter how they will later be executed, must have firm basic structures to hold them together. In animation this is especially important, since shapes have to be manipulated at all angles and distortions can easily occur. Some distortion is essential in animation, but they must derive from a basic form structure. These exaggerations should be developed without losing the original underlying shape (see Fig. 16).

Objects which are easily recognizable (spaceships or engines) should not follow photographic representation, a quality which both a live-action or still camera can do better than drawings. They should be symbols which can be visualized in two ways: (a) diagrammatic representation of the object in its simplest form, or (b) over-elaboration of an object to emphasize its plasticity. In the latter case, the plasticity of the object is highlighted and developed to the full extent. Attention can be caught by accentuating the most important points about any object. This way the drawn object can become more plastic, more realistic than a photograph, and consequently the appearance of the object will be more memorable too.

Layout

The plan which has been roughed out at the storyboard stage should be defined and fixed in the *layout*. The function of the layout is to determine in detail the precise setting of each shot of the film. Each layout should contain in clear pencil outline:

1. The shape of the objects which appear in the shot.
2. The graphic composition of shapes and forms, and how this composition is related to the movement of the objects or figures within each shot.
3. The co-ordination of movement starting in one shot so it is in register with movement in another shot.

Camera angles and camera moves (travelling, panning, zooming), should be worked out carefully making sure the elements of static and moving shapes are co-ordinated properly. One should also be careful to mark the field sizes that the camera should expose for each shot. It is easy to make a mistake here and only an exact field key would show the right dimension of a shot to be photographed. It is also at the layout stage that the film's continuity is finalized.

While the over-all continuity of a film is the responsibility of the director, the final flow of the action is defined here. The layout, if properly prepared, should contain all the essential visual information for the subsequent stages of production such as the final design of the characters, objects, animation, background and camera.

In larger studies the function of the layout and design is the work of a specially trained artist; in

FIG. 16.

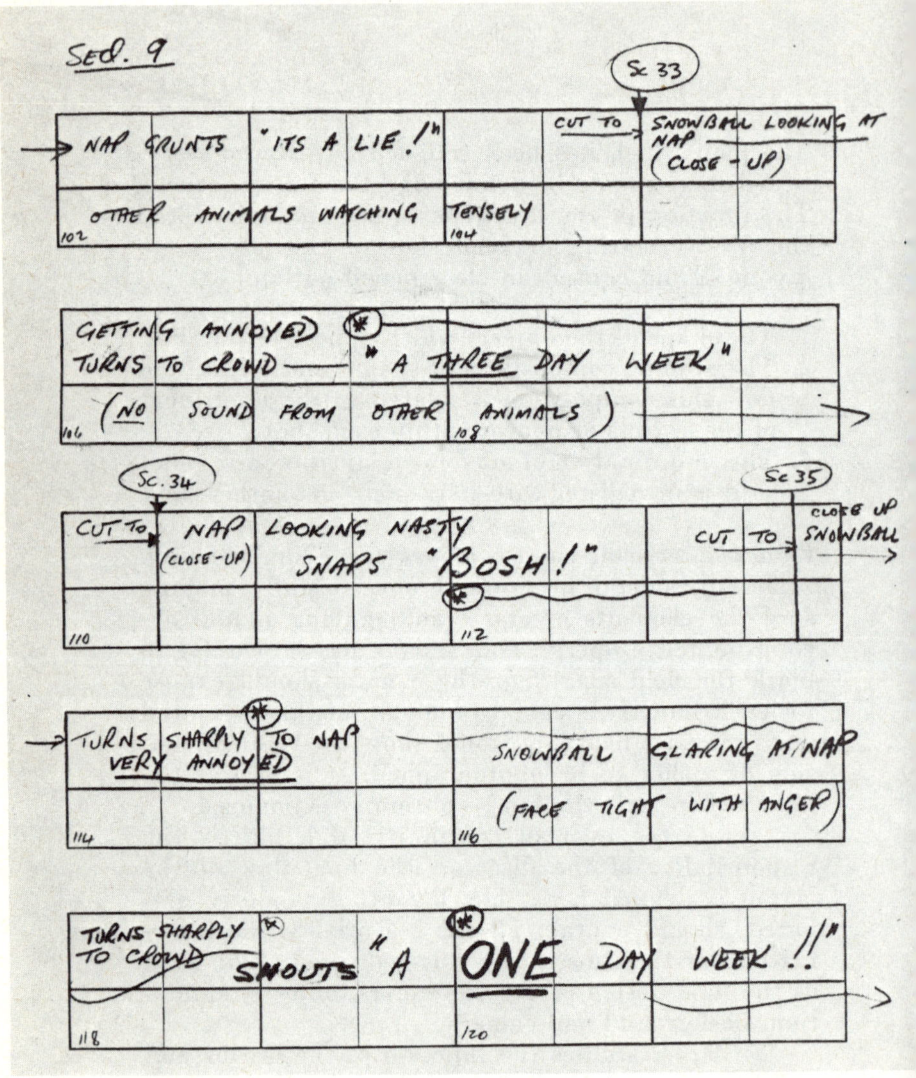

SEQ. 9

Sc 33

NAP GRUNTS "ITS A LIE!" CUT TO SNOWBALL LOOKING AT NAP (CLOSE-UP)

OTHER ANIMALS WATCHING TENSELY

102 104

GETTING ANNOYED TURNS TO CROWD — " A THREE DAY WEEK"

(NO SOUND FROM OTHER ANIMALS)

106 108

Sc. 34 Sc 35

CUT TO NAP (CLOSE-UP) LOOKING NASTY SNAPS "BOSH!" CUT TO CLOSE UP SNOWBALL

110 112

TURNS SHARPLY TO NAP VERY ANNOYED SNOWBALL GLARING AT NAP

(FACE TIGHT WITH ANGER)

114 116

TURNS SHARPLY TO CROWD SHOUTS " A ONE DAY WEEK !!"

118 120

FIG. 17. *The worksheet charts the action, dialogue camera movement and sound. It assists the production team in co-ordinating their work before preparing the final shooting script. This worksheet is excerpted from* Animal Farm, *the first full-length animated feature film in the United Kingdom.*

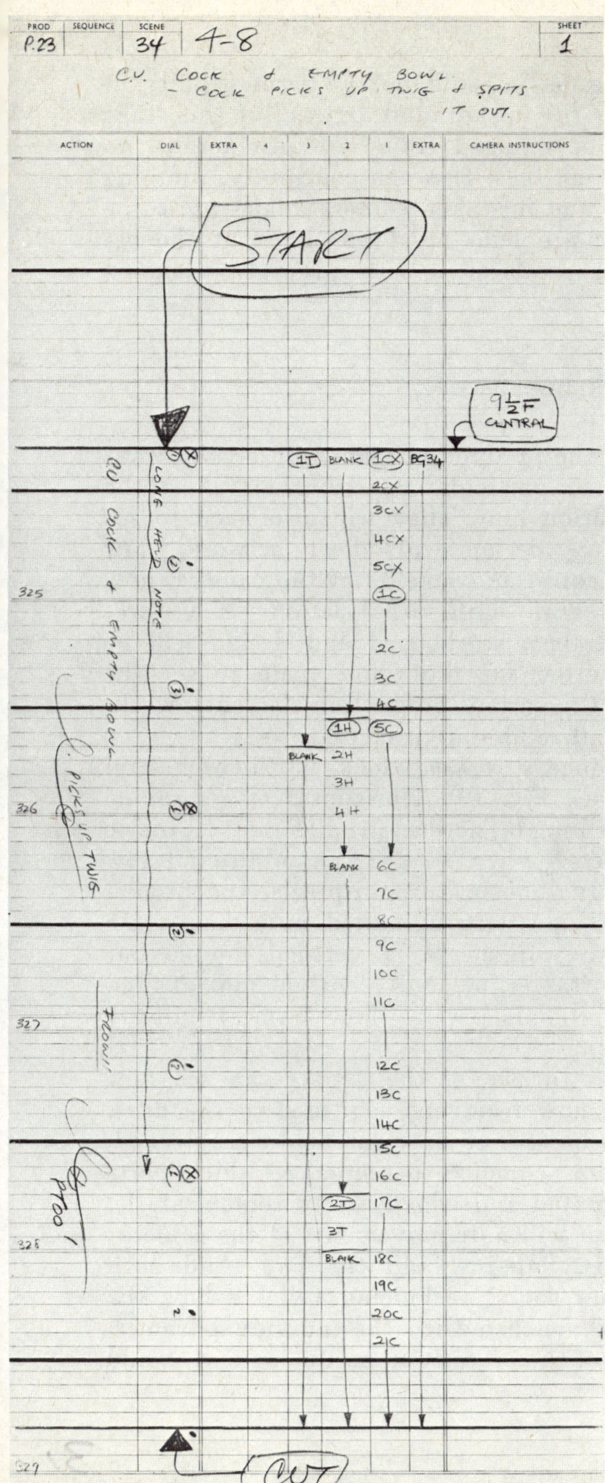

FIG. 18. *The shooting script gives precise instructions to the cameraman. It tells him the field size to use (9½F-c, or a 9½-inch centre field), the sequence of cels (1, 2, 3, 4, Background) and information about dialogue and action.*

smaller operations it could be the responsibility of the director or the background artist. But this stage itself cannot be omitted from any production, no matter how small it is. If rough continuity, jumping scene changes and mistaken camera angles are to be avoided, these problems must be solved at the begining of the production with properly designed layouts.

The worksheet

At this point, the production team will usually want to see how their particular contributions affect the over-all animation film. They will also need to see graphically how design will affect artwork, how artwork will require movements of the camera, how sound will integrate with visual action—in a word, how the treatment, storyboard and design will be executed. In order for the whole team to see the integration of the various production elements, worksheets of the entire film are prepared.

At first glance, a *worksheet* looks like an orchestral music score (see Fig. 17). Horizontal rows provide space for describing (a) action; (b) dialogue; (c) music or sound effects. When needed, an additional row provides an actual music score for precise synchronizing of music beats with animated movements. On more elaborate worksheets, a vertical double bar marks sixteen frames, or equivalently 1 foot of film. One and a half bars (twenty-four frames) indicate 1 second of film.

From the worksheet, the artists can see how their cels will flow from one sequence to the next. They will also be able to note the field sizes needed, transitions from sequence to sequence, which parts are to be animated and which are to remain static. The cameraman will note movements of the camera: pans, close-ups, fade-ins, and the like. And both cameraman and sound technician will see how the sound is to be synched with the individual frames. Each member of the production group can and should make refinements in his contribution and reach consensus on revisions, before the final shooting script is done.

Shooting script

Once the worksheets are approved to the satisfaction of all concerned, they still have to be expanded into a *shooting script* or cameraman's *dope sheet* (see Fig. 18). An animation script, however, need not be as extensive as one for a normal live-action film though it is usually more precise. Nevertheless, it should be comprehensive enough to provide information on how the action is divided into separate shots. A standard shooting script usually contains the following:

1. The field size of each shot.
2. The details of the background and the cels to be shot for each exposure; the number of exposures for each set of cels; how to sequence the layering of cels and background.
3. The angle of the camera in relation to the objects, for plastic animation.
4. Any change in the position of the camera during the photography of the shot.
5. Any movements or change in the movements of subjects.
6. The method of the photography applied in changing from one shot to another.
7. The total timing of the action.
8. Description of sound, whether it is sound effects, music or commentary, and the exact position where it will occur.

This method is useful even if the film is made by one person. But if others are also working on it, it should be possible for any member of the team to select a shot anywhere in the film and contribute his specialized skill, whether it is design or animation, and fit it in organically with the rest. Since the shooting script is the blue-print on which the whole film is built, it is definitely inadvisable to commence the production of a film until this basic work is agreed upon by all members of the team. If a sponsor is involved, he must also agree. Discussion with every member of the team can be useful as it gives the team an opportunity to acquaint itself with the subject in detail. Criticism should be voiced, carefully considered, and amendment carried out if necessary.

Sound

Closely related to the shooting script is integrating sound, whether this be dialogue, commentary, music or various sound effects. While lip synch in live-action shooting is difficult enough, synching sound in animation shooting can be even more laborious and time-consuming. In film animation, precise understanding of the film message is often dependent on strict frame-by-frame synchronization with sound or sound effects. This is specially so when animated characters are to match their movements (such as a dance) with the beats and rhythm of music.

By carefully inspecting the sound notations in the shooting script, both animator and cameraman can see how the beats of music or words of a dialogue synchronize with the visual action from frame to frame. By checking sound against artwork and camera notations, they can also note the over-all progression of action or movement within a sequence.

Continuity

In constructing the script one of the most important factors is the question of continuity. Continuity is essential to the smooth presentation of the contents of the film and to the unfolding of the story. At any given point of the film, the audience should know where they are and what they are seeing.

What should be the high point, the climax of the film? How should an event or situation be constructed? Is the time allowed too much or too little?

Can we speed up or altogether omit a shot? Are certain effects worth the effort which will have to be put into them? These and many other questions have to be answered in the script, and should be well sorted out, before the actual physical production starts. Otherwise, delays and muddle will occur to everyone's annoyance, and costs could rise as well.

Summary view of animation

To summarize, reproduction for animation involves the following ten activities:

1. Treatment and story-line prepared.
2. Character and design discussed and agreed on.
3. Layouts prepared.
4. Storyboard and rough timing worked out.
5. Worksheet prepared to see over-all flow and continuity.
6. Shooting script written with notations for cameraman.
7. Analysis of sound for synchronizing recorded dialogue, music, sound effects with visuals.
8. Animators instruction prepared (dope sheets).
9. Animation scenes are allocated to animators.
10. Background work is allocated to background artist.

These steps will be followed by the actual physical production which contains fourteen further types of activity:

1. Animation starts.
2. Line test photographed.
3. Colour models of characters and objects prepared.
4. Tracing of animation.
5. Painting.
6. Checking with backgrounds.
7. Camera chart (doping) prepared, now with specific notations and identification of cels.
8. Photography.

9. View rush prints.
10. Retakes to camera (if any).
11. Editing.
12. Mixing of sound track.
13. Negative cutting.
14. Laboratory processes.

Organizing an animation project

These steps apply to animated studios in constant production with high output. For smaller units, fewer people have to carry out more assignments.

At the other side of the scale, one may assign all creative activities to one individual and all administrative duties to another, leaving the camera work for a third person. Laboratory processing and sound recording should be carried out by professional specialized organizations.

The function of smaller organizations can be structured as follows:

1. Art activities: treatment, design, storyboard, animation, tracing, painting, background.
2. Production activities: Chartings, sound recording, doping, editing, laboratory contracts, production control.
3. Camera: time test and photography.

It is quite possible for one individual to undertake the whole function of creating an animated film. It would, nevertheless, be a gigantic task in man-hours and the production of the simplest sort of film would take far too long to complete. For this reason the production of an animated film is more suited to group activity tapping the best talents of several individuals.

Chapter V

Production of animation

With a grasp of basic principles of motion, an understanding of the possibilities and techniques of animation, we can now deal directly with production methods. This will be treated under three main headings: the animation stand, which is the workhorse of most animation production; the camera, which records the animation; and actual shooting for animation, which for artistic, professional results must closely integrate the movement of the camera and the animation stand, as well as blend the craftmanship of the animation artist and the camera man.

The animation stand

The *animation stand* (see Fig. 19) is the veritable workhorse of all animation production. It is usually called the animation rostrum, table or desk. It can be as simple as a bare table with one sturdy column for supporting a mount for the film camera and with simple spotlights attached at the sides for the necessary illumination. The camera mount is for sliding

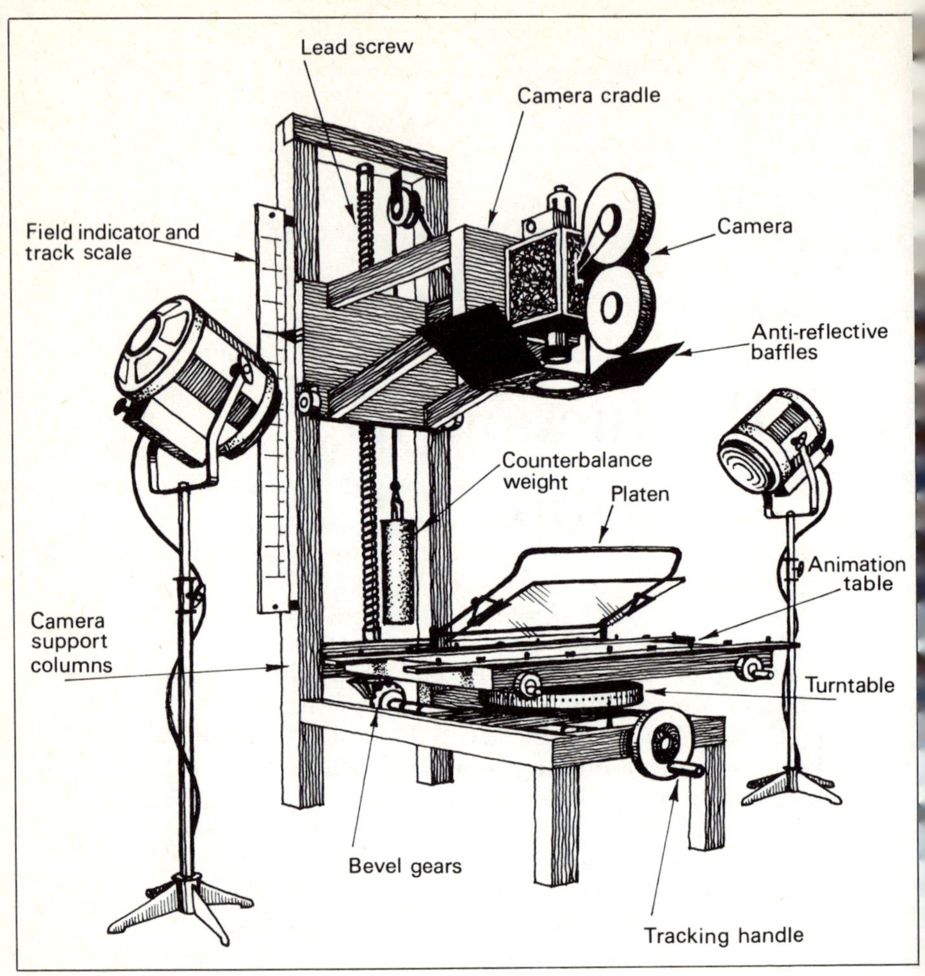

FIG. 19. *The animation stand.*

the camera up and down depending on the field size desired for the animation work. This barest of animation tables, naturally, can perform only very limited work.

The professional animation table

A more professional animation stand would have one, and more likely two, vertical columns made of ground steel tubes. A special sliding carriage for the film camera is mounted on the two tubes and driven by a vertical leadscrew operated by a handwheel. The entire carriage with the camera is counterbalanced by a weight to assure smooth and calibrated vertical movements. To facilitate calculating the distance of the camera from the table, a vertical scale reads either field sizes or distances above the table, in units of 0.01 (either inches or centimetres). If this scale marks the distances from the table, eventual familiarity with the scale and the camera lens will enable the animator to calculate the field size that the lens will expose. For convenience, he can also mark the most-often-used distance on the scale.

When mounting the camera on the carriage, it is important to assure that the axis of the lens is exactly vertical, otherwise parts of the field could be exposed out of focus or distortion may occur at the edges. One way to check the vertical lens axis is to raise the camera mount for taking the largest field size possible. A spot is marked in the centre of the field. When the camera is moved up and down, the centre of the cross lines of the ground-glass viewer should remain coincident with the spot on the field throughout the entire vertical movement.

The compound

To provide maximum flexibility of movement for animation photography, professional animation tables are mounted on a *compound*. The lowest frame rests on two parallel rails running in an east-west direction.

Fig. 20. *A complete professional animation table: an aerial image camera with computerized compound. The aerial image is a highly complex but accurate device for matching foreground animation with live-action sequences. The animation table is fitted with a self-contained process projector which is electronically interlocked with the animation camera. The live-action image is projected through a selection of lenses (like the F/e 5 Micro Nikkor or Cook Speed Pancro 50 mm f2) and a reflecting mirror to the underside of the table top. Animation cels are then put in place and shot in their sequence, always electronically synchronized with the live-action shots. This kind of a unit combines live-action photography with animation in one continuous operation on a single negative, and saves the time-consuming work of preparing travelling mattes. [Courtesy of Nelson Hordell Ltd, United Kingdom.]*

FIG. 21. *A close-up of the animation table showing the use of the turntable, floating peg bars, glass plate for rear-projection, handwheels for operating the movements of the rostrum with digital counters to show degrees of movement. [Courtesy of Neilson-Hordell Ltd, United Kingdom.]*

On top of this a second set of parallel rails is fixed in a north-south direction with a second frame mounted on these rails. This frame in turn supports the turntable upon which the animation table itself is based (see Fig. 20).

With a series of handwheels, the animation desk can be drawn in an east-west direction, a north-south direction, or rotated in a circle around the centre of the field which is also the vertical axis of the film lens. All these movements are calibrated up to 0.01 of a unit of measurement, either in inches or centimetres. This provides for the minutest movement required in animation in any horizontal direction or vertically up and down.

Travelling peg bars

In order to maintain *register* (exact positions) for artwork during exposures for animation, the desk itself is fitted with two travelling *peg bars* usually 10½ in apart running in an east-west direction when the turntable is set to zero (see Fig. 21). This allows for a field size of about 12 in or 30 cm. Three or more peg bars can also be used to permit the use of much larger fields. Another handwheel operates the movement of the bars. Between the innermost pair of bars is a glass insert for backlighting, when matteing rear projection.

These bars are fitted with movable *pegs* which keep the artwork in register. The pegs are alternately round and rectangular. The rectangular pegs are sunk into a slot in the travelling bar so that once secured, they cannot rotate. There are several peg standards, but the one commonly used is the acme standard: a ¼ in round centre peg flanked on either side at a distance of 10.16 cm by a rectangular peg ⅜ in east/west by ⅛ in north/south.

To keep artwork perfectly flat during exposure, a hinged plate glass (called a *platen*), is swung down to cover an area slightly larger than the field between the peg bars. When moving the animation table east/west, north/south, or in a rotating manner, one must be careful not to expose frames outside the largest field provided between the peg bars.

Sometimes an additional set of pegs is needed to keep one set of cels steady while another is being moved in an animation sequence, as when an aeroplane moves in a straight line from left to right against a static background. In this case *floating pegs* (a standard set of three pegs mounted on a thin metal plate) are fitted across the desk, but not attached to it. They are connected to another set of vertical columns and operated by a handwheel independently of the table. This allows one artwork or cel to be animated while the other remains static. When not in use, these pegs can be removed to provide more ample space.

Peg-hole punch

An essential accessory for the animation desk is a *peg-hole punch* for making peg holes in the artwork (see Fig. 22). The punch must be such that the holes made by it are in exact register with the travelling pegs. When punching a long cel, as for a long background pan, the three holes are punched first at one end. Then the punch is set for making only one round hole and one rectangular hole, such that the third punch merely passes through the existing rectangular hole. Such punches must be made with extreme precision, otherwise a second punching could enlarge the rectangular hole and poor registration would result.

Field chart

The *field chart* (see Fig. 23) correlates the work of the animator with that of the camera operator. It consists of a sheet of plastic, punched with holes to fit the pegs. On it a rectangle is engraved which indicates the exact size and position of the maximum field that can be accommodated between the top and bottom travelling pegs. The rectangle is subdivided by vertical and horizontal lines which indicate smaller areas within the field.

FIG. 22. *A peg-hole puncher. [Courtesy of Neilson-Hordell Ltd, United Kingdom.]*

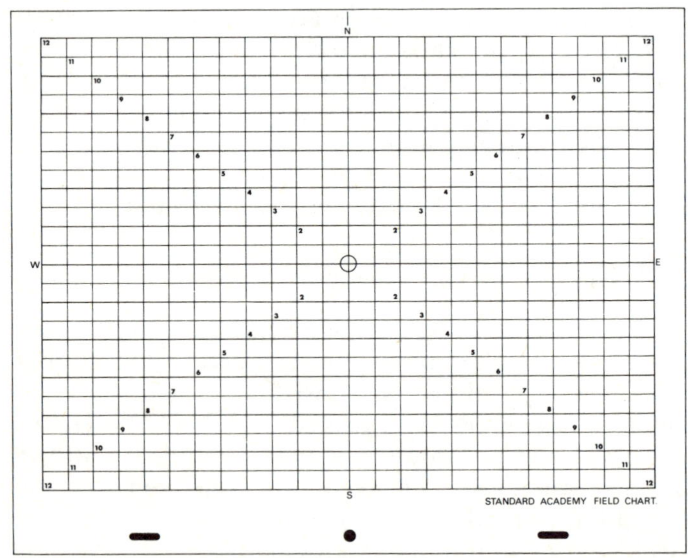

FIG. 23. *Field chart.*

Since both the animator and the camera operator have the same size field chart, the animator can instruct the camera operator on the position and size of the field to be used by referring to distances from the centre of the field. For example, 10F, 1.OE, 0.4S indicates that the field to be shot (in the United Kingdom or United States) is 10 in wide, and the centre to be shot is 1 in east of the centre of the field chart and 0.4 in south of this centre. In metric countries the same instruction would be given by 25.4F, 2.54E, 10.16S. It should be noted that the east/west and north/south instructions should always be stated in inches or centimetres, not in divisions of the field chart. Whereas the vertical lines on the chart will be in inches or centimetres apart, the horizontal lines will not, since the shape of the field is a rectangle, not a square. The position of the field centre to be shot relative to the centre of the field chart should always be measured with a ruler.

Movements of the animation desk

As can be seen from the above description of the animation desk and its components, it is meant to be a highly mobile table. Actually it is capable of five basic movements:

1. Using the sliding camera carriage, the camera can be made to approach or recede from the table, thus covering a smaller or larger field. The over-all effect would be that of a zoom lens.
2. The table itself can be moved sideways in an east to west direction or to and from the operator in a north to south direction, or obliquely by combining these two directions. This is where the compound with separately fitted frames comes into play to provide various diagonal movements.
3. The travelling peg bars can also be moved in an east to west direction allowing the entire cel to pan, while the table remains steady.
4. The floating peg bars can be moved independently of the travelling peg bars fitted to the table. This

will allow one set of cels to pan while the other remains stationary, or both cels can be panned in opposite directions, as when a character takes a long walk across the screen with a constantly moving background.

5. The entire animation table can be rotated around the vertical axis of the centre of the field.

When doing animation with movements that start or stop in the course of a sequence, it is necessary to *fair* the movement. For example, a car starting, moving, and stopping within a sequence will not be found going at 40 miles an hour from the very start and stopping dead in its tracks—although this is sometimes done for comic effect in cartoons. But even here, the movement of the car is gradually accelerated to its normal speed, maintained at that speed during its run, and then decelerated to a stop. In a cartoon, acceleration or deceleration can be greatly telescoped, but it is there none the less. In non-comic animations, the fairing must be used to prevent jerky, sudden and unrealistic movements. There are mathematical formulae for calculating the exact positions of artwork for each frame when fairings are to be used, but they are too technical for inclusion here.

More of these movements and their uses and shortcuts will be covered in a later section on production.

A modern animation stand is an expensive piece of equipment and likely to be beyond the limits of modest budgets. The alternative is to construct a simpler animation desk within the available budget. This done, the next most difficult problem will be to select a suitable camera.

The camera

If the animation work is to be shot on 35 mm, a suitable second-hand production camera can usually be obtained quite economically. The most satisfactory would be a Bell & Howell studio camera fitted with a shuttle gate. Do not accept one fitted with an interchangeable highspeed gate, as this is entirely unsuitable for animation. An alternative is a modified Bell & Howell with a Mitchell-type shift-over for viewing. This is sometimes called a 'Bell & Mitchell'.

If the animation work is to be shot on 16 mm or 8 mm, it will be very difficult to find a suitable camera short of a modern process camera specially designed for animation, and it is very unlikely that a second-hand camera of this kind will be found. The reason for this is that 16 mm only began to become a professional gauge about the same time as *mirror shutters* were introduced. Animation cameras should never be fitted with mirror shutters, because such shutters are not made to fade, and they nearly always leak light. The amount of light leaked is very small and is of no importance in live-action work where the shutter is closed only for about 1/50th of a second. But in animation, the shutter may be closed between frames for several minutes or even longer; and if a mirror shutter is fitted, there is a grave risk of fogged frames.

A camera to be used for animation should ideally have the following characteristics: (a) capability of exposing one frame at a time; (b) capability of running in reverse; (c) a gate fitted with register pins, preferably of the fixed variety; (d) a gate capable of accepting bi-pack, and a bi-pack (four-chamber) magazine should be available; (e) a fading shutter; (f) a lens capable of focusing down to very small fields; (g) a frame counter; (h) viewing through the lens must be possible, but a mirror shutter must not be fitted (the most satisfactory system of viewing is the Mitchell shift-over).

Single-frame shooting

Many substandard cameras are fitted with single-picture devices, but these are not generally satisfactory for professional work. Whether the camera is spring or electrically driven, it will depend on the motor starting (breaking inertia) and stopping (break-

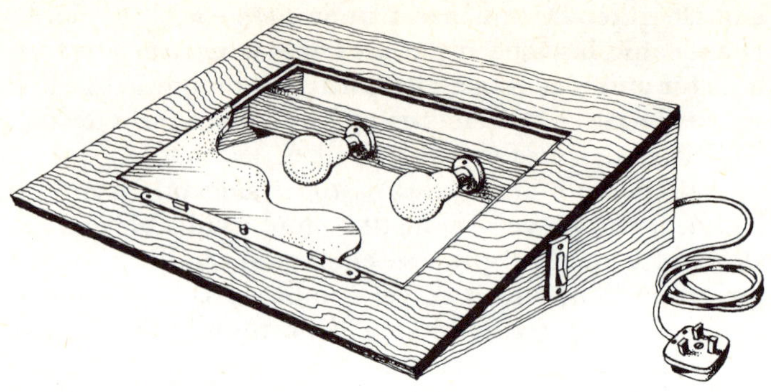

FIG. 24. *Artist's lightbox.*

FIG. 25. *A camera lens specially mounted for animation work which requires considerable close-up photography. [Courtesy of Hugh Gordon Ltd.]*

FIG. 26. *A single-picture clutch. When the mechanical finger or clutch is lifted, the notched disc makes one revolution, allowing the camera to expose one frame at its normal speed; it always maintains the same speed from frame to frame. [Courtesy of Hugh Gordon Ltd.]*

FIG. 27. *A shutter made for fades and mixes without leaking light between exposures. [Courtesy of Neilson-Hordell Ltd.]*

ing momentum) for each frame and this will generally result in slight differences of exposure between one frame and the next. Such changes of exposure, even though very small, will result in a flicker when the shot is viewed on the screen.

The older method of exposing one frame at a time is to have a continuously running synchronous electric motor, whose speed is governed by the frequency of the mains. This drives, via a worm and wormwheel, a single-picture clutch connected to the camera (see Fig. 26). At a touch of a button, the clutch will engage for one revolution and then automatically disengage itself. If this clutch is connected to a one-turn-one-picture shaft on the camera, a single frame will be exposed. Since the motor speed is governed by the mains frequency, no change in exposure between one frame and the next will take place.

However, modern electric motors are made which can stop and start each frame, and run at a constantly accurate speed, so that no change of exposure takes place. Many such motors are capable of running at several different speeds; this permits slow running when using slow film stocks and fast running when using fast stocks. Because of this obvious convenience, most modern animation cameras are fitted with such motors instead of the clutch method with a continuous running motor. In either case, the motor should be arranged so that it can be run in reverse for backwards shooting (as when shooting scratchback).

Register pins

All cameras used for animation should be fitted with *register pins*. Two pins should be fitted, one exactly filling a perforation and the other, a narrow pin which fits the perforation one way only (up/down if the pins fit two perforations on one side of the film). The best form of pins for animation purposes are fixed pins, such as those used in the Bell & Howell shuttle gate and the Newman Sinclair gate. With this type of pin, the film is lifted off the pins for movement to the next frame and then replaced. Modern animation cameras with shuttle gates are usually made so that the gates, sprocket assemblies, and magazines are interchangeable, so that any gauge can be used with the same camera.

Bi-pack magazines

A very small adjustment to such gates enables a bi-pack to be run. *Bi-pack magazines* have four chambers, two for feed and two for take-up, and can replace a normal two-chamber magazine. Usually a bi-pack magazine consists of the lower half only, and a normal magazine is fitted on top of it to provide the other two chambers. Take-up in either direction is usually done by means of four torque motors, one or two of which are energized at any one time according to the direction of running and whether single film or bi-pack is being used.

Fades and mixes

Fades and particularly mixes are very frequent occurrences in animation. These are normally done by means of a *fading shutter* (see Fig. 27). Such shutters have two blades, one of which can be moved relative to the other even when the camera is running. When they are both on top of each other, the angle of the shutter opening is nearly half a circle—it is generally 170°. When one blade of the shutter is moved relative to the other, this angle is reduced to 0°, or a fully closed shutter.

If the camera has no fading shutter, there are three other methods of varying the exposure:

1. Varying the opening of the iris diaphragm (aperture) on the lens.
2. Varying the brilliance of the lighting.
3. Varying the angle between the planes of polarization of two polar filters placed in front of the lens.

If the first method is used, the normal exposure will have to be shot at full aperture in order to give the correct exposure near the dark end of a fade, since the iris is not likely to close below f16.

The second method is suitable only for black-and-white work, since filament lamps become redder if their illumination is reduced by a rheostat in circuit or by a variac. This would not only reduce illumination but also change colour tones significantly. Even with black-and-white work, the scales used for fades and mixes will be different with differently sensitized film stocks: for example, scales used for panchromatic stocks will be different from those used for high contrast.

The third method is quite satisfactory. One polar filter is fitted normally. A second is fitted so that its plane of polarization can be rotated anywhere from coincident to perpendicular to the first (when no light will be transmitted to the lens). Rotating the filters smoothly from coincidence to right angles can make quite satisfactory fades and mixes.

Close focus

The fields used in animation are often very small, and this requires close proximity of the camera to the artwork. The lens mounts for live-action work will rarely focus close enough, though some 'pack-shot' lenses used for shooting commercials may be found to do so. In general, the lens will have to be specially mounted and its focusing scale greatly expanded so that the lens can be accurately focused at all field sizes (see Fig. 25). It is usual to fit a mechanical auto-focus, consisting of a linkage and cam system, but if this is not fitted and manual focus is used, the lens will have to be refocused for every frame of a zoom shot.

Frame counter

A frame counter is an essential device on an animation camera. An ordinary revolution counter, capable of being set to zero when required and connected to the single-picture shaft of the camera is fairly satisfactory. So connected, it will count plus (+) when the camera is running forwards and minus (—) when running backwards (such as when rewinding for a mix). When set to zero at the start of a shot, it will always indicate the frame number of the frame just shot.

Two further refinements are desirable. First, if a mistake is made during shooting, it is common practice to insert a notice 'Cut back XX frames' and then reshoot the erroneous frames. This will mean the frame counter will read (x + 1) frames ahead after the error (if only one frame of the notice is photographed). It is, therefore, desirable to be able to reset the counter to the correct number after the error. Some counters are made so that the individual digits can be reset to any desired figure. If such a counter is not fitted, it is possible to introduce a clutch between the counter and the camera, which can be freed while turning the counter to the correct figure.

Second, we have already seen that scratchback scenes are shot with the camera running backwards. The most convenient way of doing this is to load the unexposed stock into what is normally the take-up chamber of the magazine, with the taking-up reel in the feed chamber; and then have the camera instruction sheets ('dope sheets') written backwards so that the last frame of the scene is numbered 1. If this is done, then it is necessary for the counter to count plus (+) even though the camera is running in reverse. This can be done by driving the counter via a pair of 1 : 1 gears with a small gear change that allows an idler gear to be inserted between them, thus turning the counter in the opposite direction.

Viewing through the lens

As mentioned above, mirror-shutter viewing on an animation camera is unsatisfactory, and the system usually adopted is the Mitchell shiftover. In this system the camera is mounted on an L-shaped casing. The ground glass and optics of the finder are mounted on the camera door, and the lens is mounted on the front of the casting. Turning a handle moves the camera sideways on the casting and brings the ground glass into the exact position formerly occupied by the camera gate. Since the shutter moves sideways with the camera, it can remain closed while viewing, and the artwork may be viewed between the shooting of any two frames without risk of fogging. The shooting and viewing positions are accurately registered by means of spring-loaded dowels.

Lighting

Lighting for an animation stand is normally required to be perfectly flat. It is usually provided by two studio lamps (probably 750 watt 'pups') one on either side of the table. If a cel does not lie perfectly flat, even when under pressure from the platen, it may result in undesirable cel reflections being photographed. These can be eliminated by using polarized light.

Polarized light vibrates along a single plane, whereas normal light vibrates in all planes. A polar screen or filter acts as a sort of optical comb, so that only polarized light is transmitted. Polarized light that is specularly reflected by a polished surface, such as the surface of a cel, remains polarized, but when reflected from a matt surface such as pigments painted on a cell, it is depolarized. This provides a method of eliminating cel reflections.

Sheets of polaroid are placed over the two lamps such that the planes of polarization of the two are in the same direction. A polar filter is placed over the camera lens with its plane of polarization at right angles to that of the lamp. As a result, no polarized light from the lamps can reach the film. But the light reflected from the pigments is depolarized, so a proportion of it is transmitted and photographed. Thus, cel reflections (polarized) are eliminated, but reflections from pigments (depolarized) are photographed.

Shooting for animation

There are many methods of shooting for animation, too numerous to include here. But there are also a number of basic short cuts which it would be well for the beginning animator to learn. These can save time, work and material in what is essentially a time-consuming and laborious activity.

Animating a walk

This is the simplest of animation work and one in which a number of short cuts can lead to economy. Let us say that the animator wishes to have a character walk across the screen, left to right. Since a walk cycle is repetitive, the artist need not prepare new drawings for the several walk cycles. He has to prepare only sufficient drawings for one complete walk cycle. Let us suppose the character in mind is to move 2 in left to right with each step and this step is to occupy twenty frames. Then for each frame, the character must move forward $\frac{1}{10}$ in; or more specifically, the leg in motion should be animated $\frac{1}{10}$ in from one drawing to the next. If the animator decides to utilize double-frame animation (each drawing is exposed for two successive frames) then the leg of the character needs be animated $\frac{1}{5}$ in from one frame to the next. For an animated walk requiring say five complete steps to move from left to right (or 100 frames), the animator need prepare only twenty drawings. In double-frame animation, he needs to prepare only ten. If the background is to remain static with no new images introduced into it (like a bird flying across), then only one drawing has to be prepared for the background.

By using the top and bottom pegs, the animator can 'peg' the background to the bottom pegs and hold these stationary, while the character cels are attached to the floating pegs which can be adjusted to move to the right by a pre-calculated distance (for example $\frac{1}{10}$ in in single animation, or $\frac{1}{5}$ in in double animation).

Conversely, he can keep the character cels pegged steady, with the character in the centre of the field (merely changing the drawings after each single or double exposure) while the background cel which is attached to the other peg bar is moved to the left by the appropriate distance between frames. Or the character can be made to walk from left to right, while the background pans from right to left. But in this case, if the same speed is to be maintained, then the relative speeds of both character and background should be halved, otherwise the character will appear to be walking twice as fast. In the sample described both cels have to move $\frac{1}{20}$ of an inch in opposite directions for each frame.

In long walks, the animator should prepare sufficiently long cels, that is long enough for the cel to be panned for exposure without going out of frame. Of course, only the cel which is to be panned should be made long.

Shooting fades and mixes

In general, a fade is the reduction or increase in the shutter angle over a specified number of frames during exposure. Thus, a fade-in would consist in gradually opening the shutter angle during exposure, giving a progressively brighter picture. A fade-out would require gradually closing the shutter angle during exposure, thus darkening the picture.

A *mix* is the combination of a fade-in and a fade-out. It is accomplished by first reducing the shutter angle during exposure of a specified number of frames, rewinding the same number of frames, and then exposing again but this time gradually increasing the shutter opening.

A mix can be used to show a gradual scene change from one setting to another. The cameraman fades out on the cel of one scene; rewinds and changes the cel; and then gradually fades in on the new cel showing the next scene. A mix can also be used to insert effects, like a magician who makes himself invisible. In this case, the cameraman fades out on the scene with the magician present; rewinds and removes the cel of the magician; then exposes again gradually fading in on the scene without the magician.

Animating shadows

Another common use of the mix, or of splitting the total exposure between two runs of film through the camera, is the technique for animating shadows (see Fig. 28). The shadows of a moving figure are animated on separate cels and painted solid black. A first run is made of the entire set of cels including the shadow cels, but the exposures are at a reduced shutter angle, say 40 per cent open. After rewinding the same number of frames, a second run is made at 60 per cent shutter opening but without the shadow cels. The over-all picture will thus receive 100 per cent exposure, but those covered by the shadows (in the first run) will receive only 60 per cent exposure. Using this technique, the animator can also vary the intensity of the shadow by increasing the second exposure for darker shadows, or decreasing the second exposure for lighter shadows.

Superimposing titles

In the above example, the full exposure was split between two runs through the camera. It can also happen that both runs should receive full exposure. A typical example is a white title superimposed on a zoomed background. The title is painted white and is shot against a black background—preferably a cel painted black on its under side. This is double-exposed or mixed with the background scene by shooting both runs through the camera at full exposure. Indeed, in such cases, it is an advantage to increase the exposure on the title by opening the lens aperture about one-third of a stop above normal. This ensures that the title burns through any background image, but is not sufficiently overexposed to

Combined scene

Scene with shadow cels

Scene without shadow cels

FIG. 28. *Animating shadows. To animate a scene with shadows, separate cels are prepared for the shadows and painted solid black. A first run is made using both art cels and shadow cels but at reduced shutter angle. Film is rewound, shadow cels are removed and a second run is made exposing only the art cels. In this way, animated shadows appear, but allow the texture of the background to show through slightly, as it would in real life. See text for details.*

Positive of combined scene

Positive of foreground

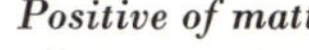

Positive of matte

FIG. 29. *Superimposition. A travelling matte allows the cameraman to mask off areas of the frame which should not be exposed. Those parts covered by the black mask (or matte) as it runs simultaneously with the raw stock can be exposed for the background scene in the second run. This will permit one image to be superimposed upon another, without one showing through the other (the effect of ghosting).*

result in halation round the edges of the lettering. Of course such superimposition is necessary only if the background scene contains a zoom which changes the size of the field. If the background scene is the same field size throughout, the title can be painted on a cel and simply registered on top of the other artwork, the whole set shot in one run.

Superimposing animation on live action

There will be times when a film-maker has to superimpose two sets of images in order to combine animation and live action in a single sequence. In this case, unlike titling, both sets of images contain colours of half tones which must not show through each other. Some examples would be the superimposition of a static spaceship over a zoomed-in background to give the impression of a landing, or animated arrows showing the flow of air in a live turbine engine. To produce this kind of effect, the film-maker can opt for either the travelling matte technique (see Fig. 29) or aerial image projection.

In brief, the *travelling matte* technique is merely the use of a negative or positive mask to prevent exposure of a shape or area on a background, in order to allow a later superimposition of the shape or figure desired. It is called a travelling matte, because the mask is run together with the film to be exposed, either in the camera during shooting or in an optical printer when exposing for the final composite print.

If the animator opts for shooting a travelling matte, the artist must prepare two sets of animated cels: one set comprises the coloured artwork cels to be superimposed, the other is an identical set of white silhouettes of the same shapes in exactly the same frame-for-frame positions. These white silhouette cels are shot against a black background on high-contrast black-and-white stock loaded into the camera with the emulsion towards the lens. This stock is then sent to the laboratory with instructions to develop for high contrast. Normal colour stock is then loaded into the camera and the colour cells are shot against a black background, using exactly the same set-up and camera movements. When the high-contrast film has been returned from the laboratory, it is loaded into the camera, emulsion to emulsion, with the as yet undeveloped shot of the coloured cels, with the matte or high-contrast film nearer to the lens. For this purpose a bi-pack magazine must be used and the camera gate must be capable of accepting two films simultaneously. The camera can now shoot the background scene. The negative matte will mask off those parts of this scene which have already received exposure of the coloured cels, and the final result will be the required superimposition without one scene *ghosting* through the other.

Shooting a travelling matte involves a considerable amount of extra artwork to prepare the white silhouette cels. It also requires a camera capable of mounting a bi-pack magazine—not always available to the ordinary film-maker. Another way is to prepare the needed mattes for optical printing. To do this, the animation cels are exposed frame by frame on high contrast stock, but using only backlighting under the rostrum. This will produce a negative matte consisting of a black background with the shape and size of the animated figure or object on clear film. Then the cels are shot again, this time on normal colour negative stock, using the same positions and timing, but with front lighting against a black background. Finally the background itself or the live-action sequence is shot separately on normal colour negative.

After developing all the negatives and printing a positive matte from the negative matte, the laboratory technician will make an exposure combining the positive matte with the colour negative of the background, to produce a positive of the background, leaving unaffected the shape of the animation cels to be superimposed. A second exposure will combine the background stock just shot with the negative matte and the colour negative of the animation cels. This second exposure will produce only the animation to be superimposed, masking off the background already shot. The stock is then processed for a composite print which will show the superimposition of the animation over the live action, both in half-tone and without ghosting.

If exact matching is required between live-action figures and animation, the cels should be prepared with the help of a *rotoscope*. This is a lamphouse fitted to the rostrum camera, which projects on to the table any developed film threaded through the gate. As the rotoscope projects the positive print of the live-action scenes frame by frame, the artist can draw the cels, precisely matching animation with live action.

Aerial image projection

The technique of *aerial image projection* is a highly technical one requiring precision equipment and meticulous craftsmanship. It is inadvisable to attempt aerial image projection, unless professionally manufactured equipment is available. Suffice it in this context to describe briefly how this technique works.

The aerial image projection technique (see Fig. 20) is a method of superimposing animation cels on a live-action sequence through the use of back projection, without the need for mattes. Below the animation table, a special register pin projector casts an image on a large diameter lens called a condensor. This condensor, whose diameter is slightly larger than the diagonal of the camera field, is fitted in place of the conventional translucent screen on the animation rostrum. Both the rostrum camera and the projector are fitted with lenses of identical focal length. This focal length is half the distance between the table top and the camera or projector lenses. Normally only one size camera field size can be used, although some systems can be devised so that either the projected field size can be varied or the camera can photograph different field sizes.

With this set-up, the live-action film is projected frame by frame on the condensor, while the top-lighted animation cels are placed on the register pegs. The rostrum camera can then shoot in sequence each composite frame of live action and animation cels.

Aerial image projection avoids the tedium of preparing white silhouettes or shooting and developing several series of travelling mattes. But it is a technique that requires precision equipment, a skilled use of optics, and carefully balanced lighting. When using either the travelling matte or the aerial image technique, exact register is essential. Both the rostrum camera and the projector for this kind of production must have register pins; prints used for projection either in preparing artwork or in shooting aerial image should be processed for low contrast and printed on a register pin step printer, on stock with negative perforation. In preparing artwork or shooting aerial image, or producing mattes, great care must be taken to assure exact start frames otherwise the two images will not match.

Shooting a scratchback

A technique that has many uses, particularly in diagram work is termed scratchback (see Fig. 30). It is used whenever a static object has to grow in the course of a scene, as for example the running out

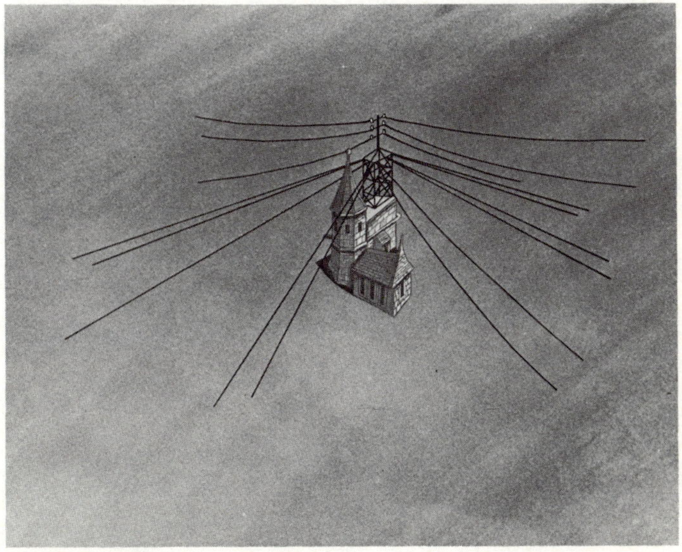

FIG. 30. *Shooting a scratchback.*

of a line or a title that writes itself as if written by an invisible hand. In such cases the completed artwork (the line of the title) is painted on a cel. The scene is shot by running the camera backwards, and a small part of the artwork is removed from the cel in each frame, usually using a paper key to indicate how much must be removed. When this technique is to be used, great care must be taken not to scratch the cel when removing part of the artwork, using either a moistened cloth or a wooden or plastic instrument such as the handle of a paintbrush. Also, artwork which is to receive this treatment should not be painted with vinyl paints which dry so hard that they become almost impossible to remove. Instead, gouache colours should be used. If the camera is not capable of shooting in reverse (which of course it should be), such a scene can still be shot if the 16-mm gauge is being used. Double-perforated stock is used and the artwork is registered under the camera upside down, and shot with the camera running forwards. When the shot has been processed, it is cut out and turned the other way up, which of course brings the last frame first and so gives the same effect as shooting backwards. If 35 mm or 8 mm is being used, this cannot be done: in 35 mm the image is not central on the film because of the space for the sound track; 8 mm has perforations on one side only, and so after turning the film the other way up, the perforations will be on the wrong side.

Chapter VI

The right kinds of economy in film animation

Economy versus quality

In general, animation work is highly labour intensive, requiring technical skills and artistic talents, plus a generous time allotment. High-quality animation also requires precision equipment which can be costly. The materials for animation need not be expensive but it would be wrong to economize indiscriminately, or in a way that sacrifices the quality or impact of a film.

Pre-production

The would-be animator is well advised not to economize in time, especially during the pre-production stages. This is where the investment in the time of artists, technicians and cameramen can pay off later in avoiding retakes, re-drawings, or even drastic change of animation techniques. The whole production team should agree on the treatment and storyboard, the selection of techniques, and the general design of the film. They should also understand and agree on where short cuts and economies can be made without sacrificing quality.

Selection of techniques

In the choice of techniques, displacement techniques (the graduated movement of semi-rigid objects) obviously require less planning, man-hours, artistic talent and camera time than substitution techniques like frame-by-frame cel animation. Against the question of economy, however, one must also pose questions of quality, efficiency, objectives and desired impact of the film.

Selection of tools

The precision registration of all artwork, whether on the artist's drawing board or on the animation rostrum is essential to the technique of cel animation. For this, it is best to purchase standard pegs and a peg-hole puncher. Cheap substitution here can only result in poor registration, jitter and distracting movement of frames and objects. Similarly, it is also advisable to have high-standard cameras that can perform with ease and accuracy all the animation work needed.

Selection of materials

As for materials, their cost depends on the technique chosen, the availability of materials and the creativity of the animator. The higher costs of cel animation are undeniable, yet there can be savings in time and materials, as was shown earlier. Furthermore, creative genius can probably discover many kinds of material for object animation by displacement and several score techniques for accomplishing this. Three-dimensional animation has yet to exhaust the possibilities of balsa, cork, soft wires, pipe wires, magnets, plasticene, moulding clay, and many other natural and artificial products available on the market.

Plastic animation requires a less complicated rostrum. Even a simple table with a curved piece of backboard to minimize unwanted shadows, a sandbox, or a simple miniature stage setting will do, depending on the type of object animation intended. One must, however, pay more attention to proper lighting angles and avoidance of shadows, calibrated animation movements of the objects, and maintaining a rigidly mounted camera.

Conclusion

It would almost seem from the foregoing discussion that any attempt to aim for high standards would rule out most savings in equipment, time and high costing skills. While this would be true for quality control cel animation (and even here there are ways of economizing), there still exists a whole range of other animation techniques requiring less equipment, time and skills.

It should be understood from the start that film-making itself is an expensive technique and animation is one of the more highly skilled arts of film-making. But one can opt for 35 mm (the most expensive in terms of equipment and film stock); or 16 mm (more economical and a number of cameras are capable of animation shooting, but one has to be selective); or in some cases, for very simple animation, 8 mm.

Naturally, it would be uneconomical to purchase a complete range of equipment and accessories for one animation film. But assuming that an organization is going to do a number of animation films over a period of years, the basic investment in first-class equipment can eventually pay off in time, quality and efficiency, particularly if the short cuts and techniques discussed earlier are used.

But it is also possible to select simpler and more economical methods of animation. Especially when using other animation methods than the finely calculated cel technique, the animator must resort all the more to his fundamental grasp of motion mechanics, call upon his innate sense of timing, and creatively interplay the choice of materials, the movement of objects and camera effects. Economy should never be an excuse for a poor animation production. On the contrary, the simpler, more economic methods require an even more ingenious use of skills and intellect.

Index of technical terms

The following is a list of technical terms used in this book. The numbers indicate the pages where these terms appear for the first time and where working definitions rather than conceptual ones are given.

[B. 10] COM 76/XXVI-2/A